WORDS OF PRAISE
for Beau Henderson and
The RichLife: Ten Investments For True Wealth

Beau Henderson is really changing the game of wealth, making us look at what living a *RichLife* really means. His wealth-building concepts are simple, effective, profound, easy to implement, and customized to *you* so you won't waste time and energy investing your resources in someone else's principles. If you want to live a truly fulfilled life, do yourself a favor and listen to Beau.

SEAN SMITH
CEO, MVP Success Systems

If you want to stretch yourself and have an abundant RichLife on your terms, Beau Henderson teaches you how to in all aspects of your life.

RON BROUSSARD
CEO and founder of Imagine!

Beau Henderson gets what a rich life really is. His radio show on WDUN has introduced us to real people and stories of how faith, family, community, and finances all work together to provide a rich life.

JOEL WILLIAMS
WDUN

Beau has the ability to take concepts that are either muddy or complex to some people and turn them into perfect clarity! We often use the phrase "know, like, and trust" as the target for our relationship with our clients. Beau has hit that target with a bullseye, especially the hardest one to earn—trust.

SHARON O'DAY

Beau is every lay person's dream! Finances are not something that people are typically experts in. Because of who you are, you give us—the everyday, ordinary person—someone to turn to for help and advice, someone we know is truly looking out for us. Such a rarity in the world of professionals! Thank you!

DENNY HAGEL

I have known Beau Henderson for quite some time now, and I can say with utmost confidence that his knowledge, experience, and understanding are second to none, and his approach to business and financial work is extremely rare. His philosophy for living a RichLife is genius and appropriate for anyone wanting to balance making money, enjoying life, and honoring your purpose. He helped me realize that my passion for being a musician could be more than a dream, and today it is my reality.

NATHAN CURRIN
Musician

In today's financial world, advisors are plentiful who claim to want to help people get back on track, but Beau Henderson is very unique in his RichLife Program by finding out what "back on track"—or a *RichLife*—means to the individual. It takes an individual who is willing to go the extra mile and provide a service when at times the only compensation is the success of the client. Beau Henderson is truly an advisor who helps his clients change their financial world and prosperity with solid core values of building prosperity based on the true laws and principles of success.

DEANA BAUM
President and CEO
The Baum Group, LLC

My words for you today are to pay attention to Beau Henderson. Go after more than just money. Chase the *RichLife*! Because you deserve it!

SANDI KRAKOWSKI
CEO, A Real Change Int'l, LLC

the
RICHLIFE

Ten Investments for True Wealth

BEAU HENDERSON

Sound Wisdom

P.O. Box 310

Shippensburg, PA 17257-0310

For more information on foreign distribution, call 717-530-2122.

Reach us on the Internet: www.soundwisdom.com.

ISBN 13 TP: 978-0-7684-0895-9

ISBN 13 Ebook: 978-0-7684-0896-6

For Worldwide Distribution, Printed in the U.S.A.

2 3 4 5 6 7 8 / 19 18 17 16 15

"Joyful is the person who finds wisdom,
the one who gains understanding.
For wisdom is more profitable than silver,
and her wages are better than gold."

—Proverbs 3:13-14, NLT

CONTENTS

FOREWORD

There are very few people who understand
not only how to manage their money—but
also create the lifestyle that they'll love.

Far too many people pursue an increase of money as if it was the answer to all of life's problems. Really, money simply is a reflection of one's life.

During the last 14 years I've had the privilege, and many times the heartache, of building businesses. While I can say that all of our companies were both six and seven figure businesses, not all increased the value of my life, gave me time and freedom, and were a dream come true. One of my companies was a multimillion-dollar corporation that was built online before even Google was created. But in 2001 it was shut down with a diagnosis from a doctor that I was so sick with multiple diseases they weren't sure what to do next.

We built a huge company on debt. I was working 70-plus hours per week, homeschooling my kids, living a "Super Woman" delusion! Eventually my body—and quite frankly, God Himself—said "Enough is enough." Selling our assets, doing the best we could to keep me alive, and dealing with multiple challenges all at the same time was not in my business plan for success.

I will never forget the day I was in the ICU with bacterial pneumonia, on two very powerful antibiotics at the same time, fighting for my life. The thoughts in my mind were not, "Oh I wish I could make more money; it will fix everything!" No, they were thoughts like, "God, if you just let me live another year, I promise to use my time wisely and stop chasing this silly pipedream."

God did let me live another year, and actually, I've been disease free for over seven years. Our finances did collapse at one point, and we lost everything we had built. But our family stayed intact, my health recovered, and the things that really mattered began to grow again. This, my friends, is when the RichLife was born for me personally.

Today I run a large company online with more than 100,000 clients all over the world. We are an information publishing company that also provides online and offline classes and events. Working less than 30 hours per week is my plan with the rest of the hours outsourced to my staff. We are completely debt free, I'm disease free, and the peace in my heart could *never* be replaced by financial increase.

We can't re-write our life as easily as we can re-write our financial future. Because of the grace of God, I have been fortunate to be able to re-write both.

My words for you today are to pay attention to Beau Henderson.

Go after more than just money. Chase the RichLife! *Because you deserve it!*

Sandi Krakowski
CEO, A Real Change Int'l, LLC

FOREWORD

After writing my book entitled *The Prosperity Paradigm*, I was asked to do several speaking engagements on the topic of money and prosperity. Most of them were at financial services events in which the audiences were comprised of approximately ninety-five percent men. But one was quite unique; I was asked to speak at a Holistic Moms Association event at a local church in Rochester, New York. Now this was the most affluent suburb in the city. These were very educated women between thirty and sixty years of age, mostly college-educated professionals who had paused careers to have children. I was the only man in the room, speaking to a group of almost one hundred women. I felt it was a unique opportunity to get honest feedback to a nagging question that men rarely answered authentically in a group setting. After being introduced, I asked the following question, and then passed the microphone around the room for answers. The question was, "What concerns you most about money?" Every single woman in the room went out of her way that night to participate. The candor of their answers was very telling. All of their responses were variations of the following sentiments about money:

1. I just don't get it.

2. The topic makes me feel stupid because the harder I try the less I understand.

3. I'm an accountant/engineer/attorney and I still can't make ends meet.

4. Though I've tried, I get confused by all the conflicting opinions of the experts.

5. I'm an intelligent individual, but it baffles me how limited I am when it comes to money.

I was amazed at the honesty these women showed. It confirmed the answers most men would give me in one-on-one coaching sessions where they could be more honest without embarrassment. These were all very bright people...some were even financial services professionals! Yet they still were struggling with feeling a semblance of control, inner peace, and confidence when it came to their finances.

As any sensible person looks at the root of the many problems facing Americans today, money is often at the core. Contradictions around money abound everywhere. People steal for it, kill for it, politicians lie for it, CEOs cheat for it, while most good people just resign themselves that "it is what it is," believing there's nothing any one person can do. That's precisely why I believe Beau Henderson has written the right book at precisely the right time.

While most books about money cover only the pragmatic aspects like budgeting or what investments to make or not to make, Beau clarifies what the rich life really is and lays out a roadmap for any earnest seeker to follow. He explores what it means to live the RichLife from several viewpoints—mental, emotional, logical, and even spiritual.

He shares a level of wisdom that I find rare in the financial world; wisdom that he gleaned through years of experience as not only a financial advisor, but as a *mentor* to financial advisors. When his knowledge is applied in the context in which it's delivered in this book, I know it will help anyone experience not only a greater ability to save and grow your money, but to cultivate something perhaps more important—economic confidence.

For the masses, the dream of being rich probably means fulfilling the desire to own lots of liquid assets like cash, homes, cars, and other material things that appear to indicate wealth. What goes unrealized is the incredible responsibility and pressure that accompanies owning and taking care of these possessions. If these things brought more pressure and created more stress, would the average person still want them? Very wisely, Beau will help you accomplish something with your money that can be done by any sensible person. That is, utilize wise stewardship with what you already have and own to experience financial inner peace.

Financial peace of mind is an achievable goal for any person committed to fiscal stewardship, and this book will help you get there. Beau beautifully explains a rare gem omitted by many popular financial books—that by educating yourself to take a principled approach to wealth creation, virtually anyone and everyone can live a *RichLife*.

Steve D'Annuzio
Founder, Soul Purpose Institute

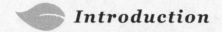

THE RICHLIFE STORY

"We must look at the lens through which we
see the world, as well as at the world we see."

—STEPHEN COVEY, author of
The 7 Habits of Highly Effective People

We are going to have a conversation about money. Some of the things I am going to say may surprise you, and some of the answers to your money problems will apply across the board to other areas of your life. Many of the things the world has taught us—about money and life—are simply not true and, even worse, eventually lead to harm. It is my intention to help set things straight.

The question of what makes a person *rich* came to me after meeting a highly respected client, a multimillionaire we'll call Richard. It was on the drive home that night, after eight years of hearing the stories of over two thousand people, that an idea began to take shape in my mind. It was a new way of looking at my job—really, at everything I do. This is the story of how the *RichLife* philosophy was born.

15

Richard was someone who in my eyes had truly made it. He was a powerful businessman who had *followed the money* and arrived, achieving business success and an enviable net worth. I was on the same path myself, following the money, so when Richard contacted me to discuss his financial situation, I offered to meet him at his house. I drove through the gates of his sprawling estate, winding through acres of emerald lawn; I parked my car, knocked on the door, and met the man who had achieved every single financial goal he ever set for himself.

I was wrong about where money had led Richard. I could see it the moment we met.

He wasn't old, but he shuffled when he walked, having just recovered from a massive heart attack. He led me through his beautiful but cold house, filled with expensive but inanimate things. We sat down in his study and we talked. Not once did he smile. He told me his story and he held out his hands. "This is what it comes down to," he said. And I looked at his empty hands and saw that everything of real value to him had been lost.

I left Richard's mansion that night in a daze, realizing that everything I had believed in up to that point simply wasn't true. It was like finding out there was no Santa Claus. A lot of people tell me their stories, and I love to hear them, but that night, a switch went off inside me. I drove home thinking about all the people I had met over the years. In particular one stood out, a client by the name of Mark whose home I had just visited a few days earlier. He, too, had come to me seeking financial advice, but instead of maximizing a vast fortune, Mark had wanted help managing his middle-class income to afford a modest fixed retirement for himself and his wife. I ended up staying for dinner, and during our meeting his adult kids and their families stopped by. There was laughter and storytelling and little kids running around, all of them so happy and familiar with one another that they were finishing each other's sentences. When I left that night, Mark held open the door and asked, "So, do you think you can help me?" Of course I said yes, but inside I was thinking, *you've got all your answers figured out. My help will be the easy part.*

Being rich doesn't just happen. It requires planning and focus; it requires decisions and guiding principles. But what most people don't think about are those guiding principles that can lead us to the greatest wealth, the greatest good, and a rich life. What I realized after meeting Richard was that I was following the wrong path. I've come to a new definition of the word *rich*. And I have put together a totally new way to approach investing.

Most people focus on the investment, but my focus is on *the investor*. Sure, I can help you find the best mutual fund or proper asset allocation, but my intention is to help you on your way toward investing *in a fulfilled life*. I've learned some of these life lessons the hard way, but with the help of amazing mentors and the wisdom of clients with sixty to seventy years of living under their belts, I have come to a new definition of the word *rich*. I'm going to take you through the steps to help you build your *RichLife*, and by that I mean becoming rich in the fullest sense of the word. I'll talk about money and life purpose, relationships and health. We'll look at managing your assets—*all of them*. I'll tell you how to get to where you want to be, how to build a safety net that will protect those assets, and how to make sure that nothing important gets left behind along the way.

This book contains 10 Investments and one Master Investment principle to help you build a blueprint for true wealth. As you go through them, I ask that you not only be open to new ways of looking at wealth, but let go of any ideas and beliefs about money that no longer serve you. Doing this will greatly increase the chances of your success. At the end of each chapter, there will be portfolio builder exercises, suggestions for what you can do right now, today, to begin putting your RichLife into motion. The good news is that there are no right or wrong answers. There are only *your* answers.

Help others achieve the healthiest, wealthiest, most fulfilled life possible.

When you identify and start living your definition of a RichLife, you begin to have a positive impact on all those around you. Working this way with my clients and peers over the years, I have become blessed beyond any success I had ever hoped to achieve professionally. Many of my clients have become my friends, some of them as dear to me as my own family. The more I share my story, the more I discover how many people are impacted by and live the RichLife philosophy. There are a growing number of financial advisors and other professionals who resonate strongly with the RichLife philosophy. They take into account the whole person, look beyond the dollar, and treat each client as a valued relationship. They have become RichLife Advisors in support of our mission.

As my dear friend and mentor Steve D'Annunzio writes, "True prosperity is being in a flow with all of life, in which the perfect thing shows up in a way that serves the need of the greatest good." Identifying and living your definition of a RichLife is the best gift you can give to yourself, those you love, and the world.

I told you there would be some surprises. Let the dialog begin.

BEAU HENDERSON, FOUNDER
The RichLife Group

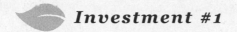 *Investment #1*

PRACTICE WISE STEWARDSHIP

"The foolish man seeks happiness in the distance; the wise grows it under his feet."
—James Oppenheim, American poet
and novelist (1882-1932)

TAKING RESPONSIBILITY

Money is an inside job, as are all things involving wealth. No matter what the asset, it had its beginnings as a thought inside you, an idea, or a desire. The desire to have a life partner, the thought that you would look mighty fine in that suit, the idea that if you can sell X amount of Y you will have the mortgage paid. It's the thought process that generates anything and everything we see in the material world. And so in order to change the way money and assets come and go, we need to change the way we think about them. The first step in this process involves the practice of *wise stewardship*.

However, *stewardship* is a term that isn't heard much these days. I admit the word sounds a little outdated. The concept is not only timeless, but wise. Closely related to *responsibility,* a life based on stewardship, or more specifically *on taking responsibility,* is one of the core principles necessary for building a RichLife. It puts the ball fully in your court, but it's important to understand the difference between being responsible and being at fault.

> "Blame implies fault; responsibility implies ownership. Blame is stagnant; responsibility propels you forward and onward to your greater good."
> —CHERIE CARTER-SCOTT, PH.D.,
> author of *If Life Is a Game...These Are the Rules*

What I'm talking about is taking responsibility for where you are right now with regard to those assets that have been entrusted to you. Now this will either come to you as good news or bad, depending on your nature. If the inner child in you balks at the thought of responsibility, consider for a moment the fable of the Goose and the Golden Egg. If you have a goose that lays golden eggs, you're not going to starve it or let it run amuck through town or, even worse, cook it. Even a child can see the error in that. You're going to tend to your goose with care because she can produce for you great wealth. In taking care of your goose, you become a steward.

Stewardship can be defined as the behavior of an accountable person. Its root word is *keeper*, meaning one who cares for and manages people and things. The careful management of that which has been given to us pertains to many facets of life, not just money. But changing the way we treat those assets, including the way we treat money, can result in a drastic and life-changing shift. It comes down to one important distinction: Do we view our talents and physical possessions as something we own and are entitled to? Or as special gifts that have been entrusted to our keeping?

LE JARDIN

Marguerite worked as a hostess for a small but high-end French restaurant owned by a husband and wife team. Because of the way they ran the register, Marguerite was not only in charge of seating the customers, but of also processing every guest check, be it credit card, gift certificate, or cash. The staff at Le Jardin was highly professional, most of the waiters career servers who had been in the industry their entire adult lives. They earned respectable incomes upward of 60K annually, working most nights, every weekend, and all major holidays. Each had their different styles of service, but there was one server who consistently out-earned them all.

On a typical night, we find Anton beginning his shift by checking each place setting. He polishes the stemware and knives; he makes sure all the settings are intact. Meanwhile his co-worker, Fernando, begins his night by looking through the reservation books. Fernando notices that a table of ten is due to arrive at six o'clock. He immediately begins strategizing ways to insure that he will get to wait on them. He talks to Marguerite about it, then to the bus boy and the bartender. He talks with the owners to find out who they are.

"They're celebrating a retirement," Fernando is told, and he turns that information over in his mind. Meanwhile, the first table arrives, a party of four, and Marguerite seats them in Anton's section. He is ready and greets them, his focus on taking them through a pleasant evening. Another table arrives, this one a party of two who is seated for Fernando, and then another four-top arrives for Anton. Now Fernando is irritated, because Anton has two four-tops while he only has a deuce. This directly affects his income because more people order more food which results in a larger bill and a bigger tip. As a new table comes in, a party of two for Fernando, he approaches the hostess stand fuming.

"I'm not waiting on another deuce," he tells Marguerite. "You're killing me!"

"But I thought you wanted the ten-top," she replies. "I'm just trying to keep the number of covers even."

Fernando runs through a quick mathematical calculation. He looks again at the reservation book and tallies the number of guests still due to arrive. He considers that the ten is a retirement party, and pictures a bunch of gray heads huddled over coffee with split entrées. Meanwhile the tables in his section wait patiently. The bus boy brings them water but they haven't ordered drinks. Anton goes by with a steaming platter of appetizers and the aroma fills the restaurant.

"Fine," says Fernando. "Let Anton have the ten-top. Just make sure that I get the six-top and the next two parties of four."

"So you don't want to take the deuce?" Marguerite asks. A nicely dressed party of four has just arrived, and Fernando replies that he will take them instead, and passes Anton the two-top. Within the next ten minutes, another party of four arrives as well as the six-top Marguerite promised to Fernando. She tries to talk to him, but now he is frantic, trying to take care of too much at once.

"How about I let Anton have this other four so you can focus on your six?" she asks. But Fernando says he can handle it. In his mind he is still working the numbers.

At six o'clock the party of ten arrives, and they are only going to be eight because one couple had to cancel. They are seated with Anton as agreed, and Fernando takes note of their age and attire. He feels good about his decision, until he notices the kind of wine they order. *Opus One! At four hundred dollars a bottle!* Fernando does some more mental math and starts fuming again. He complains to Marguerite, to the bartender, to the owners. He forgets to check back with his table of six, and so they have to flag down the bus boy who then tells Marguerite who tells the bartender who tells Fernando that they would like to order another bottle of wine. But by the time Fernando gets back to them, it's too late, and they've changed their mind.

"By the end of the night," Marguerite says, "both servers had waited on exactly the same number of people, but Anton had somehow managed to earn nearly twice the amount of money. And that small party of two Fernando passed off at the beginning of the night? They were really nice and left Anton a huge tip." She smiles. "It's like that almost every night. Fernando is a great guy. He can talk to anybody about anything. But he's always worried about who's getting what instead of just taking care of what he already has."

THE SCARCITY MENTALITY

The difference between Fernando and Anton boils down to the way they view their assets. Fernando felt he was *entitled* to the guests at his tables, whereas Anton viewed himself as their *keeper*. Anton wanted to make sure his guests had a pleasant evening, whereas Fernando wanted to insure a positive outcome for himself. Going back to our goose with the golden egg, it's the bird in the hand that counts. *There is nothing more important than the person in front of you, and nothing else you should be doing but tending to them.*

The world has been telling us since we were kids to always think ahead, watch out for number one, and be the squeaky wheel that gets the grease. Not only do we believe these things, but we behave accordingly. Ironically, thinking only of ourselves and not others has the unintended effect of pushing away the success we desire, as demonstrated by Fernando and his inattentive service.

When we come from a place of entitlement, we have a sense of being better or separate from that which we own or serve. If we go further into that, this sense of entitlement has at its core an underlying sense of unease. At the root of that unease is fear—fear that what is owed to us will be taken away, turned against us, or that someone less deserving will get it if we don't. When we apply this to our assets, and more specifically our money, we adopt a scarcity mentality. Ninety percent of the people in the world view their assets in this way. It is the sum total of what we have been told since we were children—*there is not enough, get it while you can, if you don't someone else will, money doesn't grow on trees* and so on and so forth. If you are nodding your head in agreement, as I once did, chances are you have adopted this mentality.

Once you become aware of this, you can begin to make the shift to another way of looking at your assets—physical, financial, and human. *You can become their keeper.* Adopt a grateful attitude toward who or what they are and what they are able to provide, and in so doing you will increase their productivity and your wealth.

Let's look at that statement carefully, because chances are, you won't be able to agree with it right away, let alone practice it. If you have credit card debt and receive a check that will barely cover your rent, you'll not likely be inclined to jump up and down for joy at your great good fortune. Instead, you're going to be thinking, "It's not enough. I don't have enough." In the case of Anton and Fernando, if you're watching a co-worker get what looks to you like more than their share, feelings of entitlement and resentment are going to come up. So how can you reverse this? How can you be grateful for what you have, when from your point of view what you have is not enough?

As it applies to your assets, here is the secret: the quickest way to attract more of something in your life is to appreciate what you already have. Regardless of how little or how much, be a good steward to your assets and they will multiply. Believe it or not, the laws of physics can't help but give you more. Think again about that goose who lays her shiny prize. Who will give you the biggest, most golden eggs? The bird who is loved and cared for, or the one who is feared and ignored?

WHY GOOD STEWARDSHIP GIVES GOOD RETURN ON YOUR INVESTMENT

I have more good news for you: the better stewards we are with what has been given to us, the higher the quality and the more frequent the gifts become. That's right—being a good steward will always give you a good return on your investment. Now this isn't magical or mystical or advanced economics. This happens for three practical reasons:

- First, if one does nothing to care for material possessions, they are subject to the elements, to stagnation, and to general disrepair. Like an engine that never gets an oil change, the life of those possessions is significantly shortened.

- Second, there's something wonderful that happens when you demonstrate good stewardship to others. It's called *The Law of Reciprocity* and according to psychologist Robert Cialdini in his book, *The Psychology of Persuasion*, it comes into play a majority of the time. *The Law of Reciprocity* states that if you are willing to give first, most people will be inclined to return your kindness in goods, deeds, or favors, regardless of your expectations (and for best results, you should have none). In other words, take care of the people around you, and the conditions become favorable that they will take care of you (i.e., more golden eggs).

- Third, when we respond according to the scarcity mentality, we tend to hoard, to tighten our fist, and in so doing we close ourselves off to anything good that might come our way. Even if an opportunity *does* arrive, we say *"No."* We cannot see it for what it is, because we are too concerned with getting through the month with enough money to make it. Like a sealed-off house, no sun gets through our windows, and no good news comes through our door.

ACT BEFORE YOU THINK

We see this happening every day in the lives of those around us. We all know people like Fernando, and most of us at one time or another have been that person. It is easy to become so focused on accumulating a certain amount of money or possessions that we have blinders on. The thought of stewardship is seldom considered. In fact, thoughts of others as anything more than a means to an end are rare.

But it is possible to move yourself out of this group mentality. I've seen it happen—once a person changes his mindset to a stewardship philosophy, it changes everything. It changes how that person thinks, serves, communicates, and produces. The RichLife then comes into play full-bore. This is the first step you must take toward building the life you want. Once you appreciate and care for the things you already have, you can then move on to the next step, which is identifying where you are and where you want to go.

In order to make the shift out of the scarcity mentality, you get to go against something your mother probably told you. You get to *act before you think*. (I hope your inner child is smiling now.) When that paycheck arrives, act overjoyed. Don't think about the credit card debt, the unpaid bills, or the swimming lessons your daughter needs. Look at the check in your hands and appreciate what it is before all the other negative thoughts come rolling in. Use what you have, and be grateful for every little thing it can do for you. Then apply this to every area of your life. Let's take a look at those areas now.

HUMAN ASSETS

Energy

For most people, the word *energy* applies to how we feel. There is a lack of it around midday when our eyes start to droop. Driving home from work we have a sense of being totally drained or tapped, not quite sure why as an adult we're always in such a deficit when children seem to have more of it than they can ever use up.

There is another way to look at energy. As with money, it is also an inside job. There is the physical aspect with which we are so familiar, but there is also a larger force at work—the thoughts we think. That's right—*our thoughts are full of energy*. Even before we act on them they affect our physical being. You are either creating positive or negative energy through and by your thought patterns. Believe it or not, it comes down to science.

The study of quantum physics has determined that at a sub-atomic level, an atom is either a particle or a wave. These waves are invisible, and we know them as energy. Everything in the universe, including our thoughts, begins with energy in one form or another, and according to the scientific study and observation of these atoms, matter (particles) and energy (waves) are attracted to that which is of a like vibration. This means *you attract what you put your energy and focus on*, consciously or unconsciously—whether wanted or not. This is the basic precept of the Law of Attraction.

It has been proven scientifically that thoughts are energy that can actually be measured. So take a moment to ask yourself, *how do you measure up with respect to being a steward of your thought energy?* Are you allowing negative thoughts to have free reign? Do you have fear, anger, resentment, jealousy, and bitterness that often occupy your mind? If so, it can be a prime example of poor stewardship and a massive drain on your energy.

Most people don't even realize how negative they are. In fact, over half of most people's thinking tends to lean toward the negative and fear-based. It's surprising how much more energy will become available to you once you become aware of this inner drain.

The late Dr. Masaru Emoto is a scientist most known for his study and photography of water. Given that 71 percent of the earth's surface and three fourths of our bodies are made up of water, Dr. Emoto conducted groundbreaking research documented in his book, *The Hidden Messages in Water.* The study provides stunning conclusions about the effect of our thoughts on physical reality. The doctor's work was visually presented in the documentary film *What the Bleep Do We Know.* Maybe some of you remember the scene where they set up glasses of water to visually record the effects of negative energy. Participants in the study were asked to approach these glasses of water and direct specific thoughts at them. After a designated period of time, profound results were visually available and put on public display.

When my friend, Claire, saw the film, she was impacted most by the visual difference between the two extremes: the glass of water that received hateful words—accusations, judgment, and blame—was literally black and murky. The water glass that received positive encouragement and gratitude remained crystal clear and on a molecular level was beautiful to look at.

Claire realized then she'd gotten into some negative habits of blaming and complaining, and inspired by the film, she decided to conduct a study of her own: she would go for one full month without complaining. She marked the days out on her calendar and kept a journal to take note of any physical changes she felt. Near the end of the month, I asked her how things were going, and with a wry grin she confessed, "I have to be very quiet."

Claire went on to explain. "Every time I get together with my girlfriends, we talk about our husbands or boyfriends and we complain. I know that sounds terrible. We don't do it in a malicious way, we just commiserate. Talking would dissipate my negative feelings, and afterward I would feel better. I think it did help at first, but then I noticed it was becoming a pattern we had fallen into. We would bring up old stories or expect things to go the way they had gone in the past and we weren't letting the energy go. We were keeping it alive by talking about it over and over again, the same old things. I would talk to my friends, and then afterward I would be all churned up about something that had happened a long time ago. Sometimes I would even be anxious about things that might happen, things that weren't real at all. It affected the way I thought about and behaved around my boyfriend. So, I decided to keep my mouth shut. My girlfriends and I went through an awkward period, because basically I had to re-train my brain. But the relationship between my boyfriend and I actually improved."

It was two weeks after that conversation my friend Claire announced her engagement.

Thoughts of complaint and blame require a huge amount of mental energy, and in the end nothing good ever comes from them. Problems solved in this way are temporary bandages, harsh words aimed at someone else in order to boost our own self-image. Most complaints are not intended to solve problems. They are not even directed at the people with whom the problem occurred. When Claire realized her complaints to her girlfriends were not only misdirected but also a drain on her energy, she stopped doing it. She found that a better use of her energy was to become more proactive. She began looking for the things that were *right* instead of wrong and discussed any concerns with her boyfriend first. Doing that helped them both move forward, and she became an example to her girlfriends. In fact, despite their awkward period, even those relationships deepened as they became drawn to her positive energy.

Now, retraining your brain might not sound like a fun thing to do, but I guarantee you it will produce surprising results. All the anger, bitterness, and resentment that you feel you have a *right* to hold on to is harming only you. Not only does that rob a person of physical energy, it contributes to a wide variety of illnesses as well.

It creates and releases more and more negative energy that, in turn, attracts more negative people, unhelpful events, and lack of assets.

> Worrying actually helps to create the very things you are trying to avoid.

In the case of Claire and her girlfriends, their discussions perpetuated strong negative feelings about the men in their lives that prevented those relationships from growing. In terms of our finances, this is how poverty and scarcity thinking keeps people in a continual pattern of lack and insufficiency. Even if at first you can't change those negative thoughts, just becoming aware is a huge step toward becoming a good steward of your energy.

Time

We human beings have gone to great lengths to invent machines and systems designed to save us time. As a society, *time equals money* is a mantra we all believe in. But what, exactly, have we done with all the time we have supposedly been saving? Tasks are often dragged out and expanded to fill a certain time slot. This is as true for the hourly-wage employee as it is for the entrepreneur as it is for the retiree. It is especially true for directionless individuals who have not yet discovered their life purpose. Their days are filled with tasks that have nothing to do with the purpose and calling of their life. Because these tasks are often energy draining, efficient use of time is not possible.

We will spend a great deal of time talking about life purpose in the next chapter, but as it applies to stewardship, a good rule of thumb to apply here involves becoming aware of your own authentic response to offers that will require your time. Jack Canfield, author of *Chicken Soup for the Soul,* explains it this way: "When you are presented with an opportunity to do something (say someone has invited you to be an officer of your favorite civic club), if that opportunity doesn't excite you so much that it causes you to say, 'Hell yes!' then by default, the answer for you is most likely a 'Hell no!'"

Even though this is said tongue in cheek, the guarding of our precious energy is something that needs to be looked at. Time is finite. There is only so much of it in any given day. A directionless person will say yes to most anything and everything. The focused person, on the other hand, is well able to say no because they are able to prioritize. You will find that you are either spending your time moving toward or away from your purpose. This does not mean that you are involved in *bad* pastimes or *wrong* activities, but rather it means that you are involved in things that are not helpful. These things are at the expense of investing in what is best for you and for your life purpose.

If time is given away randomly, with no direction or purpose, you won't have any left to invest in the things and areas most important to you. It helps to remember that we are all given the same number of hours in every day. What you do with those hours will become more and more clear to you as you further develop your plan for achieving a RichLife.

Life

Your life purpose is rooted in the gifting and talents that have been endowed to you. We will spend the next chapter on life purpose, how to identify it, and how to invest in it. But for now, one of the most basic ways to learn your life's purpose is to ask this question: "If you could spend your days doing what you love, regardless of whether or not you received monetary compensation, what would that thing be?" The answer to that will most likely reveal valid clues toward what you were put here on this earth to do.

Once you have identified your life purpose, put it to the question we brought up earlier with regard to stewardship: Do you view your talents and physical possessions as something you own and are entitled to? Or as special gifts that have been entrusted to your keeping?

When you view your life as a gift to the world, it makes sense to take steps to insure it. Later on in the book, we will talk about the importance of taking good care of your body. We hear advice over and over again from doctors, surgeon generals, and mothers, but you're going to hear it from a financial planner. If you have been prioritizing money above taking care of yourself, it's time to set the order straight. We are talking about your assets, and because *you* are the most valuable asset you've got, *you* come first.

When it comes to finances, you are your most important asset, not the stacks of printed paper. You are the one with the ability to earn. Life insurance is something most often sold to us out of a fear-based mentality. We buy it because we are afraid of what will happen if we don't. For those of you who have resisted the idea of life insurance for this reason, or for those who feel they can't afford it, I offer a new way of looking at it.

Insure your life for its full value, the same way you would a home or car. Doing so shows good stewardship of your most valuable asset, *you and your earning potential.* It is easy to believe that you can't afford it, but this way of thinking buys into the scarcity mentality, and the idea that money is more important than the people it was created to serve.

Purchasing life insurance also demonstrates good stewardship for the people most important to us—our family and loved ones. One of the most touching stories I ever heard came from a woman named Lynne who called in to the radio station during one of my talk shows. You could hear the tears in her voice as she told me about her husband, Arthur, who had died a few years ago.

"I didn't know anything about what insurance policies he had taken out. But after he died, the life insurance he bought allowed me to pay off the mortgage. That was so important to me. This was so important because I live on a fixed income. He gave me peace of mind," she explained.

It takes most of us our entire lives to realize that peace of mind is an asset. You don't have to wait that long. You can realize it right now.

Relationships

My grandma used to say, "Birds of a feather flock together," and it's true. We do emulate those with whom we spend time. It might be time to ask yourself why you spend time with the people you do. Often we spend more time at work than with our family and friends, because we have convinced ourselves that the goal of accumulating money is more important. I've seen it time and time again how that goal leads to a hollow and unfulfilled life. The *business first* mentality, or the *end justifies the means,* results in an erosion of our most important relationships, both friends and family. And it does nothing to build a healthy environment among the people we work with.

Relationships are so important, I'm going to spend an entire chapter on it later in the book, but for now, with regard to stewardship, ask yourself the following:

- What kind of steward are you to the people closest to you? Are you investing in carefully building those relationships?

- Outside of family, do you spend time with those who bring out the best in you? Those who encourage you and challenge you?

- Are your group of friends made up of people who scoff at your dreams and visions? If so, you may want to consider finding a new group of friends

33

In a later chapter, we'll take a new and different look at how to build your team of professionals. Imagine surrounding yourself with like-minded professionals such as financial planners, accountants, attorneys, life insurance agents, trainers, and coaches. In other words, begin looking for individuals who are living their life purpose—mission-driven professionals—who are passionate about what they do. They will value you as the customer above the transaction and in so doing will offer you a higher quality of service. But it goes even beyond that. Aligning yourself with these types of individuals will also help you move toward your RichLife.

My experience with mission-driven individuals began shortly after the night I met Richard and began to redefine my idea of rich. It happened almost organically when I began telling others my story. I saw that there were already people out there who took great joy in their work because they were really helping people. And they were some of the highest paid, most respected professionals in their field. As I began talking with them, I heard their stories, learned the how and why of what they do, and as a result I became influenced by them in a positive way. Many even went so far as to give me a hand up. These are the people you want to look for as you begin to build your RichLife team. There are hundreds of financial advisors in my area who can help you set up an IRA. But a mission-driven advisor is really invested in the client and adding value to their life. These are the kinds of professionals you want to make it a point to do business with.

How we treat the people who are closest to us affects our peace of mind. So, too, do the interactions we engage in on a day-to-day basis. If we make it a point to be kind to everyone we meet and to patronize those businesses that do us the greatest service, we are showing good stewardship toward human life. In turn, we will receive more of it for ourselves—more energy, more self-worth and peace of mind—and nothing helps fuel our life purpose more, helping us to be more productive or creative, than peace of mind.

PHYSICAL ASSETS

Stuff

I have a friend who travels for her work and so she spends a lot of time in airports. Juli is of slight build and so is often approached by others offering to help carry her bags. She always politely refuses. "I believe a person should pack no more than they can carry on their own. That's my rule, and I keep by it. That allows me to come and go as I please, without having to wait around for anyone to help me. That's especially important if you're a woman travelling alone," she explains.

We all have a certain amount of physical possessions, some more than others. While it's important to care for and be responsible for what we have, it's also important not to place an inordinate amount of emphasis on physical possessions. As the old saying goes, it's better to "own our possessions" and not "have our possessions own us." Too much value placed on possessions is a one-way street to disappointment and lack of fulfillment. If you ask a person at the end of his life if he wished he'd purchased one more boat or a bigger house, that's not usually at the top of the list.

Stewardship in this respect has as much to do with priorities as what we do with what we have. A lot of people don't consider caring for their things a priority. They either don't have the time to perform the maintenance work and so just keep buying new, or they simply don't care. This second could be due to a lack of energy. Sometimes, we really don't have the time to keep up with maintenance issues at home, or we really did pack too much stuff. We then have two options—either hire someone to help us, or downsize to something we can handle on our own.

A colleague of mine has a son who is learning piano. His teacher, an accomplished musician in her own right, told him that as a general rule, when playing a piece of music you must never play the piece faster than you can play the most challenging part. In other words, the difficult section of the song dictates the tempo of the entire piece, because that difficult part must be managed securely. This is a good analogy to apply with possessions. You want to be sure that they do not own you and that they do not take up too much of your energy and time.

> As a rule, take on no more than you can comfortably manage in the pace of your day-to-day life.

If you have to slow down for one challenging part, say for example, taking care of a house that is bigger than you need, then the entire song of your life will suffer the consequences.

FINANCIAL ASSETS

Money

The very item that most would consider to be first in the list of being a good steward actually comes last. So often I see individuals who justify spending all their time at the office because they are "climbing the corporate ladder." They feel that by earning more money, they are taking care of their family. The end result amounts to dollars accumulated in the bank and with a deficient family life. The miserable multimillionaire I mentioned at the beginning of this book is a prime example of why money must not come first. He had alienated his family to such an extreme that none of his children were speaking to him by the time I showed up to help manage his fortune. He was also on his third marriage. I later found out from his lawyer, however, that she had just served him his divorce papers.

Sudden Wealth Syndrome

Most people have bought into the equation that the world is selling: *money = happiness.* It's simply not true. We have erroneously given pieces of paper a weight and value higher than that of the people it was meant to serve. If money were all it took to become happy, we wouldn't have the malady known among professional counselors as "Sudden Wealth Syndrome." The money finally appeared, but then in most cases, the happiness disappeared.

Sports stars, entertainers, and lottery winners are notorious for making a great deal of money in a short period of time and squandering it quickly. They start spending it on things that only go down in value (mansions, yachts, cars, jewelry, and partying) and start to disperse the remaining money on things that have no personal value. They can usually keep this up until they stop earning the big money or, in the case of a lottery winner, until they run out of capital. I could give dozens of examples here, but let's just take a quick look at one—former NBA star, Latrell Sprewell. Sprewell purchased a 5,200-square-foot, 70-year-old mansion with six bedrooms and four fireplaces. He purchased it as a home, though he was hardly in it, and eventually couldn't keep up with the expense of a $920,000 loan. Because Sprewell failed to make the monthly mortgage payments, he lost first the $1.5 million yacht, and finally the mansion. Both purchases good examples of poor stewardship.

There are many statistics that show how Sudden Wealth Syndrome affects various people in various ways. Many of them end up saying they wish they had never won the money in the first place, and they are dead serious when they say that.

Context of Money: Good or Bad?

Some people get stuck in financial ruts because of a belief they hold, most of the time an unconscious belief—that money is *bad*. To want it, to have too much of it, even to pursue it is considered wrong. We've all heard of the expression, *money is the root of all evil*. Well, this is another myth I would like to help dispel, and here is another secret—money by itself is neither good nor bad. Money by itself is neutral. It is what you do with money that becomes either good or bad, right or wrong. The *context* in which the money is used has nothing at all to do with the money itself and everything to do with the person using it.

Think of the people who are closest to you. Picture them standing with you on the shore of a wide, moving river. On the other side of that river is a picturesque island with houses and trees. On the shore behind you is a raging forest fire.

Now people are running and jumping into the water. It is pandemonium all around, but you spot a man at the marina selling rafts for a thousand bucks. If you buy a raft, you can put your family on it and get them safely across the river. Many people are trying to swim, but the current is too strong and they do not fare well. You have a thousand dollars in your pocket and as the flames roar behind you, you think, *what a great deal!* You gladly pay the thousand dollars for the raft. You put your family on it, and off you go toward safety.

Once installed on the island, you are so pleased with the performance of this raft that you pick it up and carry it with you everywhere you go. You know it has great value—it was expensive and saved everyone in your family—and you will not let it go for anything in the world. It is very heavy, and you work hard to keep the raft safe. You strain and you sweat; some days you really become stressed about it. Meanwhile a drought comes. The riverbank becomes muddy and the water unsafe to drink. Drinking water becomes scarce and very expensive, and those close to you start to become sick.

A group of men offer you bottles of water in exchange for ferrying their cargo across the river. They have a dark look to them and you are suspicious of their intentions. You discover their "cargo" is not only water but women and girls, and you realize they are traffickers. But still you ferry them once a week, under cover of the night, because they pay you water and besides, these are desperate times. You do this work until your wife finds out. She begs you to sell the raft but you won't. She refuses to drink the water you bring home and eventually becomes very sick. Still, you won't part with the raft.

News comes from downriver that an artesian spring has been discovered, flowing freely from a cliff side. You find out the name of the town and, though it is nearly 300 miles away, you immediately set off, determined to bring back gallons of water for your loved ones. You know you must keep the raft safe and in good repair to hold all the water you will be bringing back. Trouble is, as you make the journey there are storms and turbulent waters. The raft becomes your entire world. You stop often to make repairs. You work hard to keep it safe. When the town with the spring finally does show up, you float right on past it, busy with your raft. The river becomes wider, the current stronger. You cling to your craft and eventually you become directionless, at the whims of the current. When you finally do embark upon shore, you are thousands of miles away from your family, and you have no idea where you are.

The raft in this story represents money. Like money, it is a vehicle to help you get from here to there. Its value came from its ability to get you to where you wanted to be, and like money its value increased depending on the number of people it was serving. On land, it wasn't worth very much. On water, it was worth a fortune.

So the question is, was the raft good or bad? The answer is that it was both. Its value depended on how it was being used. The raft was good when it saved your family. It was bad when it caused you stress. It was bad when used to harm others. It was good when it set you on your way to find better resources. And it was bad when you became so focused on it that it distanced you from what you valued most. When we apply this idea to money, we call it context.

When thinking of the dollars in the bank or in your pocket, view them in terms of context. Consider those dollars in terms of how they are to be used and how they will help you get to where it is you want to go. View them in terms of the good they can do for others. It is also important to note here that money earned in a way that harms others will in turn only harm yourself. But the converse is also true—money used in the service of others will only increase and help you to become more prosperous. It all depends on context.

The purpose of this book is to help you achieve the richest life possible, and by that I mean that I want you to have full access to all the assets—human, physical, and financial. You may be surprised by what comes first—*you*. You may have also noticed what comes last—money. That's right, you are the greatest asset you have. In the next chapter, we are going to get to the core of your life purpose. Once you identify that and bring to it the practice of wise stewardship, you are well on your way to receiving one of the highest returns on the best investment there is.

PORTFOLIO BUILDER

Being a good steward means taking care of or being a good keeper to what you already have. It is the first essential step toward achieving financial success, and if practiced consistently good stewardship will bring positive returns on your investment as soon as *right away*.

THE TAKE-AWAYS

- There are three kinds of assets—human, physical, and financial. It is important to show good stewardship over all your assets, not just money.

- As it applies to your assets, the secret to attracting more of them in your life is to appreciate what you already have.

- Act before you think; to make the shift out of a scarcity mentality, make a conscious effort to be grateful for any and all assets currently in your life. Act before you think, and appreciate what you already have.

- Money is neither good nor bad. Money by itself is neutral.

- The value of money is based on context or how it is used.

ACTION STEPS

Make a list of all the assets in your life. Write down the things you can begin doing in each of those areas *today* to demonstrate good stewardship. Perhaps the greatest physical asset we have is the one right under our feet. Make it a point to practice good stewardship toward the planet you live on. When out in the world or even in the office, pick up any litter you see, even if it isn't your own. You can begin doing this right away, indoors or out. When I used to go camping with my dad, he always made us stop and take a look around before we got in the car to go home. He would ask the question, "Am I leaving this site better than when I found it?" If the answer was "yes," then we would go on our way.

Being a better steward of our "spaces" is something you can easily begin doing today. But be sure to make a list of future goals, things you would like to implement down the road, and work out a realistic time frame for achieving those goals. Here are a few examples:

- **Stewardship of Time:** Think about where and how you spend the bulk of your time. Time can be budgeted the same way that money can. Try charting your days for a week or so and see where the "time leaks" exist. Are your minutes and hours spent on the mundane and meaningless? Or are you investing that time in areas that will result in long-term benefits to you and to the community at large?

- **Stewardship of Stuff:** Maintenance of your house or car can be time consuming, but putting it off will only insure that it will cost you even more in the end. Make a list of the small maintenance tasks you have been putting off, and come up with a workable plan to get them done. For example, involve the family in house projects and regular car washing. Schedule time for regular oil changes, maintenance checks, and tune-ups for all the engines you rely on. (Don't forget the snow blower!) When things need to be repaired, take them in to a professional right away instead of waiting until the problem gets so bad the repair turns into a replacement.

- **Stewardship of Money:** Good stewardship of money puts the emphasis on context and the person it serves. As it applies to your RichLife, you want to invest in yourself first—your life and where you are going. Apply the principle of paying yourself first. This discipline teaches you to live on less than you have coming in. A certain amount of every paycheck is set aside and put into savings. I recommend having this deducted automatically if you can. The amount is up to you and will depend on your individual financial situation. It doesn't matter if it's $5 or $5,000; what's important is that you get into the habit of doing it. Other good examples of wise stewardship with money would be to invest in your education to further a career and/ or to raise your financial IQ, working with mission-driven financial advisors, investing in tools to start your own business or books to increase your knowledge. Make a list of those investments that can begin to serve you rather than the other way around.

- **Bonus Gift:** Download your free copy of the Action Guide for *The RichLife: Ten Investments for True Wealth* at www.RichLifeActionGuide.com.

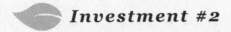 *Investment #2*

CLARITY

"Most men lead lives of quiet desperation and
go to the grave with the song still in them."
–Henry David Thoreau

As I said at the beginning, a RichLife doesn't just happen. It requires planning and focus and a set of guiding principles. In order to get what you want, you must first get clear about three things—what you already have, where you want to go, and how to get there. In this chapter we are going to make three investments in clarity. We are going to talk about your life purpose, your definition of a RichLife, and the goals and objectives necessary to fulfilling your purpose and achieving your RichLife.

1. LIFE PURPOSE: YOUR GIFTINGS AND TALENTS

Maybe you have a pretty nice house or apartment, a car that takes you to work, and a toothbrush that belongs to someone you care about in the slot next to yours. Maybe you have a decent life

45

with some money in the bank and a little left over to go out to dinner now and then. But still, you know that something isn't quite right. Deep down, you have a sense of unease. The sense that you aren't *doing* enough or, more accurately, *that enough isn't being asked of you.*

That sense of unease, feeling like you still have something left to give the world, is important to listen to. It's important because there is a reason why you are here. Each of us has been given a unique combination of gifts and talents, of interests and desires, that no other human being has. When followed, that combination has something particular and great to offer the world. Thomas Edison once wrote, "If we did all the things we are capable of, we would literally astound ourselves." The time has come for you to begin astounding yourself. The time has come to identify your life purpose.

Some people might have an idea of what their talents and gifts are because over the years they've come up, but for one reason or another they have suppressed them. Maybe it wasn't what your parents expected of you, or what a boy or girl of your social standing should consider. Maybe there simply wasn't anyone around you doing anything like that, so you didn't even know it was possible.

Perhaps you are one of the few who *have* identified your gifts and talents, made half-hearted attempts to bring them to the forefront of your life, but never quite made it.

Still there are others who don't have a clue.

Do you recognize yourself in any one of these scenarios? Now, here's one more: those who are tuned in to their life purpose and go after it with all they're worth, without regard to the opinions of others and in spite of their own personal fears. They set out to do what they feel compelled to do, and they seem to have enormous vats of energy to do it with. Because their life purpose becomes their focus as opposed to the accumulation of things, these people are in the process of becoming good stewards of their energy. They have the physical and mental stamina necessary to complete their task and to fulfill their calling and so eventually, they get there. And when they do...these are the people who are the most fulfilled in life. These are the individuals we read about in our history books. They are the ones who know what they are all about and what they do best.

The Quest

After seven years of dedication and practice, Karen Armstrong had to admit to herself that being a nun just wasn't working. It didn't feel right, and no matter how hard she strained and worked, she had to admit that she couldn't get to the places of joy and gratitude that she believed were possible in the life of religious service. So she left. It was an excruciating decision to make as a young girl of twenty-three. One of the most frightening things for her was the idea of having to support herself once she was out in the world. Karen thought her failure in the religious life meant she was through with religion altogether. She wrestled with many fears, but in the end, she found the courage to embrace what came naturally to her. It was a process of discovering what her life was all about.

After leaving the convent, Karen spent several transitional years during which she earned a degree from Oxford University and wrote about her experiences as a nun. The resulting book, a deeply candid autobiography, *Through the Narrow Gate,* led to an invitation from British Channel 4 television to write and present a documentary series about Saint Paul. Though she had doubts about her abilities to do such a thing, Karen accepted the job, and so began a new adventure.

It was during the intense research and study necessary for the writing of the documentary script that Armstrong began to experience feelings of limitless joy. For the first time in her life, she literally jumped out of bed every morning because she couldn't wait to begin working. The intense scholarly study required for the job wasn't really *work* for her at all, but a glimpse of what the Benedictine monks call *lecto divina,* or divine study. What made it divine for Armstrong, however, was the passion she had for what she was doing. After she finished writing the television series, other assignments followed, and all of them concerned religion. She writes:

At first my new involvement in religion remained on an intellectual, critical level. But as I went deeper into the history of religion, I began to experience that sense of being on a quest that had impelled me to become a nun and had kept me in the convent for all those years. It was different, of course, because I was an older and—I hope—wiser person this time around.

What she had discovered this time around was a portal that eventually led her to discover her life purpose. Karen Armstrong is now one of the world's most beloved and respected interpreters and authors of religious faith today. Yet she had thought she was done with religion forever. It is interesting how some part of her felt called to the study, though it took her years to figure out just what her particular niche was. She had to first admit to failure in the convent before her success elsewhere in the world could be found.

That *sense of being on a quest* is what you are looking for. Even if until now you have never given it any thought, it is not too late to begin. There are *no fast tracks* to success when it comes to our life's work here on earth, and no one who knows any more about it than you. What I can tell you, however, is that the feeling of being on an important and valuable quest—feelings of joy and excitement at the beginning of your workday—are possible. And it is not just possible for a chosen few, but for everyone.

The Vital Question

Remember the question set forth in Chapter 1: "If you could spend your days doing what you love whether or not you received monetary compensation, what would you do?"

The something that came to your mind as you answered that question is something you can spend time doing for hours and never grow weary. On the contrary, it creates energy! This something makes you feel alive, valuable, and excited. If you know what that is, you are on the right track.

If you don't know, think back in your life to those times that were the happiest for you, the times when you experienced the sensation of being complete or fulfilled. Or, the days when the time just flew by because you were so absorbed with what you were doing. What *were* you doing?

There was a time in Julia Child's life before she was *the* Julia Child. This was depicted in one of the more charming moments in the film *Julie & Julia* during a dinner scene in which Julia's husband asks her what she really likes to do.

"What do I like to do?" she repeats. "Well, I like to eat! I mean, just look at me! I'm getting bigger by the minute!"

Think back also to those times when you were the most miserable. What do you dislike doing? What causes you stress or feelings of anxiety? Take a moment to figure out why you disliked it.

The clues are there. We only have to follow them.

Follow the Clues to Your Purpose

By evaluating your passions, your values, and the basic skills that you were born with, you will begin to find the clues to your purpose. Here's a short exercise that I use with those who attend my seminars. Grab a pencil and invest a few minutes of your time right now and see what you come up with. You might be pleasantly surprised! Remember, you're looking for clues to your own personal life purpose. In the same way that every plant grows from a seed, so, too, your life purpose will grow from what is already inside of you.

Answer the following questions off the top of your head. Try to respond with the first thing that comes to you. If, after later reflection, you wish to go back and change some of the answers, you may do so, as long as they resonate with authenticity. In other words, be honest with yourself here.

List five things you are passionate about. Whenever you are engaged in these activities, time just seems to *fly by*.

1. _____

2. _____

3. _____

4. _____

5. _____

List the times in your life when you were the happiest and experienced the highest level of fulfillment. These might be memories from your childhood, moments with your grandparents, or times with friends. These happy memories can be anywhere, not just at the work place. Think about what it was that you found so fulfilling.

1. _____

2. _____

3. _____

4. _____

5. _____

List five (approximately—there may be more or less) skills and talents that you feel are innately yours and that you were born with. It might not be that you were instantly good at these things, but rather that you had an inexplicable need or desire to do them. In other words, it didn't matter whether you were good or not, you enjoyed it. It might be that in the repetition of the doing, you got pretty good. It might have been said at one time, *"Hey, that kid's got talent."*

1. _____

2. _____

3. _____

4. _____

5. _____

List your five top values. These are the things that are important to you, the codes you live by. Ask yourself who you admire, or who you most look up to, and think about their character traits if you need clues.

1. _____

2. _____

3. _____

4. _____

5. _____

Make a list of the people and professionals who you think could benefit from the skills or talents you identified above. *This part is important,* because life purpose isn't just about identifying what you do, but who those gifts will serve. Ideally, this will help you on your way to identifying your market.

1. _____

2. _____

3. _____

4. _____

5. _____

Our life purpose may not at first seem very grand. And on another note, not all of us are cut out to be celebrities or world famous historians either. Your life purpose may be humble, your preference one of anonymity. In working with my clients, it often seems that those people with more evolved souls often prefer to live more simple lives, in supporting roles rather than in the spotlight. All that matters here is you seek to get to the root of who you are and what you really like to do.

Fear Factor

So now you've got your lists. They have helped to shed some insight, given you some clues as to what you already have and what you are here to do. But if finding a person's life purpose was this simple, more people would be living it out on a daily basis. Once you have an idea of your gifts, the basic, most common roadblock to living them to their fullest potential is *fear*. For some people, one of the biggest clues to their life purpose is that it *is the one thing they are the most afraid of doing*, because for them it is the one thing that matters the most. To help get a little perspective on our fears, consider what is asked of health care workers worldwide who minister daily to patients with highly infectious diseases.

All in a Day's Work

It is just after sunrise in West Africa, and a young nurse we'll call Janjay dresses carefully for work. She kisses her four-year-old daughter, Mardea, goodbye, and says a prayer before leaving, "Please, let none of my family get Ebola."

As a nurse, Janjay took an oath to save lives, and so she travels to one of the pop-up hospitals throughout Liberia known as ETUs, or Ebola Treatment Units, operated by the International Medical

Corps. Before entering the hospital corridors, Janjay puts on several layers of protective gear that cover her completely from head to foot; a co-worker writes her name in marker on the outside of her mask. "I cannot sit at home all day knowing there are all these people who are suffering," says Janjay. "This disease more than any other takes away human dignity. Even if I cannot save them, I can at least be a voice to them in the dark."

The nurses who work in the ETUs do some of the most dangerous jobs, inserting intravenous drips, taking blood or cleaning up body fluids, all of which make it possible for them to contract the deadly virus. Ebola shuts down the kidney and liver functions of patients, so painkillers cannot be administered. In the most rural areas of Liberia, ambulances drive for hours to fetch and carry patients to the nearest ETU, and teamwork is required to transport the patients safely.

"They know they are risking their lives," says Janjay when talking about the team she relies on, "so we all do our best to do things the right way." This is especially important to Janjay, who gets sprayed down with disinfectant several times a day. The suits can only be worn a few hours in the intense African heat, and removing them is considered the most dangerous time, because coming in contact with even a drop of body fluid can mean contagion.

"I think of my children," says Janjay, "and all day I think of them, and how I would want them to be cared for if they were the ones who were sick and in suffering."

At the end of the day, when Janjay goes home, her children do not hug their mother or even touch her until she has washed her hands, showered, and changed clothes. The Ebola outbreak in West Africa has to date claimed thousands of lives, but it has clarified for Janjay her life purpose. "We are not just nurses or doctors or patients. At the end of the day, we are all just people."

While the above story uses fictional names, the facts accurately reflect life during the Ebola outbreak that hit West Africa in 2014.

Fear can bring a clarifying directive to our life's purpose. If what you wanted to do most in the world could potentially endanger you or the people you loved, would you still want to do it? Why? What are the fears that are holding you back from achieving your life's purpose? And are those fears real, like the Ebola virus, or are they imagined?

Fear comes in many shapes and sizes, but as it applies to life purpose, the most destructive manifestations I've noticed are feelings of *not enough*. These are the fears of not *being* enough, *doing* enough, and not *having* enough. This fear of not enough is the foundation for many of the world's most successful marketing campaigns, and unfortunately it has become so prevalent in our culture it may be at the very core of our own reasons for doing or not doing without us even knowing it. Let's take a look at some of these "not-enough-isms" right now to see if they apply.

Using your list created above, choose one of the things that you are passionate about but not currently doing. Fill in the first blank of each sentence with what you have chosen, and complete the following "not-enough-isms." (Feel free to tinker with the wording of your sentence if necessary.)

Being enough: How does what you think about yourself affect what you are willing to try or not try doing? How does what you think about your appearance affect the way you behave? The risks you are willing to take?

I can't _____ because I'm not _____ enough.

(*Example I can't run a marathon because I'm not young enough. I can't become district manager because I'm not educated enough.*)

Doing enough: Who are the people and what are the circumstances in your life preventing you from doing what you want to do? These are excuses cleverly disguised as obstacles. Once you identify what is in your way, you can begin talking to these people and looking at the situation to see what can be done.

I can't _____ because of (person) _____.

(*Example: I can't go back to school because my husband isn't spending enough time with the kids.*)

I can't _____ because of (situation) _____.

(*Example: I can't do an internship because I'm already working two jobs.*)

Having enough: What are some of the things that are missing from your life that may be preventing you from doing what you would love to do? Are these things missing simply because you haven't identified that they are necessary, or because you have a genuine inability to acquire these things? What will it take for you to begin acquiring those things now that you've identified them?

I can't _____ because I don't have enough _____.

(*Example: I can't be a writer because I don't have enough room in my apartment for an office. I can't take night classes because I don't have enough time or energy and I'm always exhausted by the end of the day.*)

Sacrifice Versus Service

To take a chance at making a life instead of just making a living may seem to some like a very risky thing to do. We have had the fear of not having enough for retirement drilled into us for years. We also have the fear of *not doing enough* for our children reverberating in our ears. These "not-enough-isms" are the fears that keep us stuck in the mode of a scarcity mentality, and they prevent us from going after what we really want in life. Many of us are convinced that the best thing we can do is to focus our efforts on high-paying jobs, regardless of their personal value to us, so that we can earn enough for our retirement years and earn enough to send our kids to college. We cling to jobs we don't find fulfilling in order to keep the job benefits, the 401(k) and the retirement funds. We are taught to sacrifice our own desires and talents in service to the futures of our children and the security of the retirement years. There is another way to look at the work you do—a way that allows for both service to others and fulfillment of ourselves.

What I have learned with regard to retirement and self-sacrifice is that it leads to non-fulfillment. It leads to an incomplete life. Putting all your eggs in the money basket for a grand retirement someday does not lead to balance and happiness today. Remember Richard, the miserable millionaire? And with regard to sacrificing our passions and talents in the interests of our families, here is the mindset that will be the most helpful to develop:

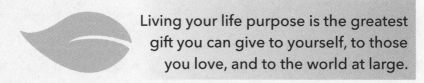

Living your life purpose is the greatest gift you can give to yourself, to those you love, and to the world at large.

This is what God created you to be and do, and there is no legacy more powerful to leave behind for your children than a life well lived. Become a living example to them. It takes courage and determination to move against the grain, but it's well worth all the effort required. It's an exhilarating feeling to know who you are, what you are all about, and how you can contribute the most value to self, family, community, and the world around you.

The RichLife principle is built upon the concept that we are responsible to ourselves, and to the community at large, to invest in and live out our life purpose in the best way possible. Discovering your life purpose has nothing to do with age or the stage of life you are in, and it is better discovered late than never at all. In fact it's amazing how much can be accomplished in a short amount of time when one's inner passion is lit up and on fire. The energy that gathers when you are doing what you are meant to do enables one to change focus completely. It gives a person the courage and strength to break through all of those chains of fear. I've seen it happen in numerous instances, and I've heard numerous stories. *I have seen clients make more money in their retirement years than ever before because they are finally doing what they really want to do.* Why wait until you retire to do what you really want to do?

Mixing Your Gifts

I have known Nancy and her family for a little over a year now, but I've always noticed she has a very vibrant creative streak. Like Janjay, she also works full time as a nurse while raising her family, but Nancy has always had a deep love for music. Instead of waiting until her retirement years "to finally do something" with her musical gifts, Nancy found a way to marry two seemingly different worlds.

On two separate occasions, Nancy has been able to revive previously non-responsive coma patients through effective playing of her violin, particularly the vibration of the A note. The last time we met for lunch, she had just gotten the necessary certifications to develop a music therapy curriculum at the hospital where she works. Imagine how thrilled she must be to utilize both her medical knowledge and her love of music to improve the lives of her patients. This is a wonderful example of how following your gifts leads to improvement in the world. You don't need to wait. And you don't even have to quit your day job!

With regard to life purpose, here is the secret: once you have identified your gifts and talents, the most direct way to securing success is to use them in the service of others.

Now I'm not saying to give your labors away for free. You should be financially compensated for what you do. What I'm saying is that the attitude you have as you go out into the world is one of value creation. You work with this end in mind—*not* the paycheck, but *creating the most value for others.* If you work with clients, your focus is on meeting their needs exactly; if you are a craftsman, your focus is on building things of quality and beauty that will improve the lives of others.

Do you see the difference? Again, this is an inside job. This is a new approach to work, and it requires a new mindset, but I guarantee you that the results in the quality of your life in areas both personal and financial will be dramatic and life-changing. You are the greatest asset you have. There is nothing more you need in order to start identifying and putting into place your life purpose. You are enough. Using the gifts and talents you have with an attitude of service to others will propel you to eventually become one of the most respected, highest paid professionals in your field.

Imagine right now what it would feel like to wake up refreshed and enthused about the day ahead of you. You literally can't wait to begin work because it is fulfilling, challenging, and of great value to others. Furthermore, you respect and enjoy the people you work with and for, and you are paid well to do this work. In fact, though it has taken you a few years, this enjoyable work has now become the sole source of your income.

Flash forward ten or twenty years down the road, and you have become so skilled at this work, so sought after in your field, that you are now at a place where you are financially secure. Secure meaning that you have all your bases covered, proper asset insurance, and risk transfer. Protection against erosion factors, such as inflation, market volatility, and taxes. Now imagine that all along the way, you have set aside time for the people and activities most important to you. Because of this, you still have a sound body and the presence of loved ones. The stereotypical idea of retirement is really not necessary. You're having a great time! Contributing to society and completely in charge of how you spend your time, you have no desire to quit so you can do what you really want to do. You *are* doing what you really want to do! And as your priorities change, you are able to adapt and shape your life accordingly.

This is where I am leading you. This is my definition of a RichLife, and it begins with you.

I can't wait to see where Nancy's music takes her, and I am so glad she didn't wait until retirement to find out what she could do. When it comes to the stories I have heard from my clients, the thing that strikes me most is the fact that no one ever says, "You know, Beau, I really regret doing this or doing that." They never say that. What they regret are the things that they *didn't* do. And the ones with no regrets are the ones who *won't* die wondering.

Don't Die Wondering

It was opening night of a highly acclaimed play in a small off-Broadway venue. The cast was exceptionally talented, the crew was tight, and the rehearsals during tech week had all gone smoothly. The director of the play was an established, well known and respected professional in the theater community. He had recently been interviewed for *Dramatics* magazine and had won a prestigious award. The house had sold out, and everyone was in good spirits, anticipating a great review and a long run. But before curtain went up that night, the cast and crew were called into the theater. And it was there that a confession was made.

Timothy stood alone up on the stage. He was wearing his usual boots and a pair of jeans, with the black leather jacket the cast had seen him arrive in to nearly every rehearsal. But for opening night, he had a large button pinned to the sleeve of the leather coat. The button was a dirty yellow, pretty battered, and in bold black letters it read: **Don't Die Wondering.**

"I have called everybody here tonight to tell you my story," he began. "I have been a director now for ten years, working my way up from the grad school plays, little by little, and I am thrilled to be here at this venue with you tonight. But you should know that ten years ago, I was lying in a ditch in the rain, too bombed out of my mind to even walk home."

The entire room became still. This was their director speaking, a distinguished man somewhere in his early fifties, who had lead them fearlessly through eight weeks of rehearsals. He had been clear and insightful, at times even eloquent. No one could picture him as anything other than who he was now. But he went on. It was clear from the emotion in his voice that the story was difficult to tell.

"I was a drug addict, unable to hold down a job, and I had pretty much alienated my family and anyone who tried to help me. That night was probably the lowest point of my entire life. I spent the night in that ditch, in the rain, and I was waiting for a reason to come to me. A reason why I should bother getting up. I couldn't think of one single thing. So I closed my eyes and just let it rain.

"The only thing I was ever interested in was the theater, and everyone who ever cared about me told me it would never pay the bills. Told me it wasn't the place for me. So I believed them. I got myself into a respectable line of work, one that could support my wife and family. By the time of the night in question I was so miserable, spending the night in a muddy ditch felt preferable to returning to my life. And for some reason, I started thinking about this play I had read way back when I was in fourth grade. I had found *Death of a Salesman* in the library, just picked it off the shelf, and I read the whole thing that afternoon while I was waiting for my dad to pick me up. And I remembered thinking, *God, I would just love to see this story come to life.* Lying in the ditch that night, I started wondering what would have happened if I'd followed that. I was lying there thinking about that play, and when I opened my eyes, I saw this button, lying there in the mud. This button right here."

He thumbed the button pinned to his jacket. The one that read: **Don't Die Wondering.**

"And I saw what it said, and I went, all right. All right then. Because in the end, that's all it comes down to. Either you die wondering what would have happened, or you go and find out for yourself. I picked up this button, picked it right up out of the mud. I picked myself up too and checked into rehab. And ever since, I haven't looked back. It's been hard. But I keep this to remind me, and I'm telling this to remind you. There isn't anybody else you have to answer to."

2. DEFINE YOUR RICHLIFE

We are now going to complete the foundation for the new structure that will become your RichLife. You have uncovered your hidden talents and desires, you have a clearer idea about your life purpose, and you know what you want to do. You have also identified some of the obstacles that have been preventing you from doing that. We are now going to take that information and move toward building your RichLife from where you are standing right now. We are going to make a few more investments in clarity by identifying *who, what, when, where,* and *why* in regard to your definition of a RichLife. Because now that you understand how to honor your life purpose, the next thing you'll want to do is paint the picture of what a fulfilled life looks like to you. This picture will become your definition of a RichLife.

Who, What, When, Where, and Why

I first got into the business of financial planning after the premature death of my father. My mother suddenly found herself in completely new territory, and she needed someone she could trust, someone to help her sort through all of the money jargon. She had some important long-term decisions to make for herself now that the picture of her life had changed. I found the job of helping her to be both challenging and rewarding, and comprehending financial terms and current tax laws came easily to me. I had found my area of life purpose, and I set about learning everything I could.

Years later, I was a full-fledged financial advisor with a long list of clients I enjoyed helping. But I was pursuing the wrong thing. I was running clients through a system, focused on seeing the required *number* of people needed to hit my income goal. I was so busy and so goal-oriented in regard to the number of people I saw that I was no longer spending the quality time required to *really get to know them*. I was just trying to keep up with what I had made the year before, but with that as my focus I was losing enjoyment for what I was doing. My daily life became a grind and I felt conflicted with regard to my values.

I was not living my definition of a RichLife. So, too, it was with Karen Armstrong when she was living the religious life in a convent, feeling miserable. Living your RichLife will involve utilizing your giftings and talents in the service of others, but it will feel *good, joyous, and right*. It will be in line with those values and principles important to you.

RichLife by Design

We are now going to get clear about the small things. Simple things like where you would like to live and what time of day you work best. Maybe you are a baker, but aren't suited to working in the wee hours of the morning. For you, life as a pastry chef in a night restaurant might be a better fit. For Karen Armstrong, immersion in religion did not mean living in a convent. I, too, had to take a step back and get clear. To look at the bigger picture of *why* I loved the work that I did and *what* was missing.

For me personally, what I found to be of the most value as a financial advisor was helping others get to where they wanted to go. It didn't matter to me whether those goals were financial or otherwise. I like to see people on their way toward doing, being, and having more of what makes them fulfilled and happy. I now have a team of people who work with me. I meet and check back with the clients I coach every six months to make sure they are keeping on track with their RichLife. By connecting with people the way I was meant to, as opposed to focusing only on the numbers, my relationships deepened and my income increased. In other words, when I stopped focusing on the money, I actually made more.

I had to look at *why* I wanted to be a financial planner in the first place, and then restructure my business so that *what* I did and *how* I worked reflected the why. We are going to take that step now with regard to your RichLife. We are going to start with the small things and work up to the big.

Now, I want you to picture what your RichLife looks like. What is your definition of happy and fulfilled? Honor the preferences that you have, and your RichLife will come into focus.

Start with a completely blank slate, with no regard to how any of this could be possible given your current circumstances. Pick a time 5 to 10 years out into your future, and imagine what you are doing. See yourself there, doing it. Ask yourself: Where are you? Who are you with? What time of day is it? What are you doing and why?

Once you can see the scene clearly, take a moment to record the answers to the following questions:

1. Who are the people I want to spend time with?

_____

_____

_____

_____

2. What gives me joy and satisfaction?

_____

_____

_____

3. What do I want to be doing on a daily basis?

_____

_____

_____

4. Why is this important to me?

_____

_____

_____

5. When, or what time of day, do I best perform?

_____

_____

_____

6. Where do I want to live and work?

_____

_____

_____

7. What is my definition of a RichLife?

_____

_____

_____

_____

3. MAKE IT HAPPEN

Designing your RichLife and living out your life purpose is an inside job. It requires you to be clear about who you are, what you do, and why. It requires that your focus be one of creating value for others, including a quality life for yourself. Living out your RichLife doesn't happen just because you want it. And it certainly won't happen if you don't start taking steps toward it. A lot of people make the mistake of waiting *"until they are ready."* This is another "not-enough-ism" disguised as an obstacle. You do research and write business plans, take class after class, but never feel *ready* enough. Don't wait for that magic moment to arrive. Start now. Every one of us has something to offer. It doesn't matter how much or how little you think you have, the only thing preventing you from moving forward in this area is yourself.

With regard to your RichLife, here is my prescription for success: get started right now. That's right. Don't wait until the kids are in college, until you have enough in your retirement account, or when the economy changes. By the same token, I'm not telling you to run out and quit your day job, either. Remember Nancy and her violin? There are things you can begin doing right now to move toward making a greater living. Some of those things will be small; for others great changes will take place. Everyone will have their own obstacles, their own time frame, and their own pace. What's important is that you identify your RichLife and begin to make plans that will move you toward, not away, from your fulfillment. You do that by beginning right now, with what you have.

Going back to the idea of good stewardship, you take a good look at the positive assets around you, focus on what you have instead of what is missing, and then use that as your starting point. Everybody has to start somewhere. And as the saying goes, the years are only going to go by anyway.

What Have You Given Up for Others?

Charis at one time in her life sang professionally, and music was a part of her every day. Singing was definitely her passion. But then life happened—as it so often does. Nearly two decades went by with Charis fully immersed in family life, work life, being a diligent wife and mother. After her son went off to college, Charis's marriage fell apart. At a time in her life when it seemed that the sun had gone out, Charis rediscovered her love of music. She turned her attention inward and discovered that though her gift had been forgotten all those years, it was still a part of her. And it still had the ability to bring her joy.

Fighting through her fear, Charis approached a neighborhood restaurant and offered to serenade their clients for free. That idea expanded, and now she does the same thing at several other restaurants on the weekends. Will this venture turn into a paying proposition? Perhaps. But for now, Charis is thrilled beyond words at the opportunity to once again have music back as a central focus her life, and to sing for the pure joy of singing. It has given her confidence during a difficult time in her life and brought her a sense of inner fulfillment.

Remember our basic question? "If you could spend your days doing what you love whether or not you received monetary compensation, what would you do?"

Charis knows exactly what that is in her life. She rediscovered what she had given up for others once those people in her life had gone. She was able to turn things around for herself by reconnecting to that part of her life. It doesn't matter how old you are or how far away you have gotten from yourself. Your gifts and talents are still there, and they are part of you.

What Could You Be Doing Now?

Akiko's day job is in corporate America, but you only have to talk with her for a short while to discover that her heart is in her painting. Her name is Japanese for "bright child," and even as a small kid she loved to play with color. A few years ago, Akiko realized that she was wasting precious time by thinking she had to wait until she retired to be able to enjoy her art. She set up a studio down in her basement and began to devote more and more hours to what she loved doing. At first, it was only an hour or two on the weekends. Then she found a way to fit painting into her daily routine for forty-five minutes. The paints were all set up and everything she needed was there. She was able to efficiently budget her time, and eventually, little by little, that time began to add up.

She sold a few pieces of her work to encouraging friends, and then to a local gallery, which served to boost her confidence and confirm the direction she was taking. She invested the money from those sales in a subscription to *Art Journal* magazine and art classes, and continues to get a little bit better every year. In the back of her mind, Akiko is always thinking about and planning for that next painting, and it gives her great joy and satisfaction. In fact, she has more energy for her day job in corporate America and recently received special recognition.

As Akiko nears retirement, she does so with the knowledge that not only will she have more time to paint, but she will have the skills and the discipline in place. She is so thankful she didn't postpone getting started, and she has already seen great improvement. Even though it seems she never has enough time to paint, it still adds up. And during the busy times of the year when she isn't able to get to her art at all, knowing there is a project downstairs waiting for her through. She gets to fulfill her purpose in the *now* of her life, instead of waiting for a future that may never arrive.

What in Your Life Has Changed?

David came to me a few years ago for advice in the real estate market. He had worked for years as a carpenter with a local construction company, and he wanted to invest in some real estate properties himself. The idea was to fix up the properties and then rent them out for income. He had an exact goal in mind. The magic number was $3,000 a month. When I asked David if he was setting this up for his retirement, he said, "Heavens no! I've just decided what I want to do with my life!"

David's RichLife is a little different from that of Charis and Akiko. A new person arrived in his life a few years ago, a sweet little granddaughter by the name of Kayla. Because of the situation with Kayla's parents, David now feels his RichLife is to spend as much quality time with his granddaughter as possible. He wants to fully be a part of her life—being there with her and for her as she is growing up, being the person she can go to and talk with about anything. This is what makes him happy; this is what makes him feel the most fulfilled as a person

The exact definition of your RichLife can go through many metamorphoses. As your values and priorities change, a shift in the design of your life may be necessary to reflect that. Answering the questions of *who, what, when, where,* and *why* in regard to your RichLife is something to continually reevaluate as you grow and evolve. Adjusting your definition of a RichLife is part of "growing up." The twenty-year-old who wanted to live in the big city, performing with theater troupes and never settling down, may now be the forty-year-old who wants to write her novel and raise a family in the country. David's granddaughter is still a toddler, so this definition of a RichLife for him is a fairly recent development. When his granddaughter is grown and on her own, his definition will shift again. This is why it is never too late to identify your life purpose and begin nurturing that. It is never too late to design what a RichLife looks like to you.

RichLife Goals and Objectives

Now that you've done the work of identifying your life purpose and getting clear about what your RichLife looks like, you have guidelines and a starting point. The key to success is to begin now. Clear goals and objectives are the vehicles that move you toward your RichLife beginning today.

In each of the following seven areas of your life, identify one thing that you can do that will take you one step closer toward your RichLife. Be specific. List how much and by when for each goal. In other words, *the goal must be measurable.* For example, in the area of health and fitness, don't write: "My goal is to be skinny." Write: "My goal is to weigh 153 pounds by January 31, 2016 at 5:00 p.m." In the area of finance, don't write: "My goal is to make a lot of money next year." Write: "My goal is to be making $100,000 by December 31, 2016, at 12 midnight."

Warning: There are two things to be aware of in regard to goals and objectives. First, make sure that whatever you prescribe for yourself is in line with your definition of a RichLife. Keep to the compass of your values. And second, don't become so attached to the goal that you lose enjoyment for the process and sight of what you are accomplishing. If you are striving to secure two new clients a week, eight new clients a month, and you only get four in the month of December, that's still four more clients than you would have had if the goal were not in place. Keep at it. Reward the progress. In the next chapter, "View Life as a School," we'll take a look at why all failure is necessary and how you can turn every mistake around and use it to your advantage.

Job/Career

- My goal in this area is to _____

  _____

- How much? _____

- By when? _____

Financial

- My goal in this area is to _____

  _____

- How much? _____

- By when? _____

Recreation

- My goal in this area is to _____

  _____

- How much? _____

- By when? _____

Health and fitness

- My goal in this area is to _____

  _____

- How much? _____

- By when? _____

Relationships

- My goal in this area is to _____

_____

- How much? _____

- By when? _____

Personal

- My goal in this area is to _____

_____

- How much? _____

- By when? _____

Contribution

- My goal in this area is to _____

_____

- How much? _____

- By when? _____

 PORTFOLIO BUILDER

Determining what you can do today to begin living your RichLife has deep and far-reaching rewards. Living a RichLife doesn't necessarily mean an extravagant lifestyle, owning a big mansion and a yacht, and traveling the world. It all boils down to what is important to you. Being a good steward of your life purpose means taking steps now to identify and develop your giftings and talents. This is a choice that only you can make. By staying current and making investments in clarity, you get to be the designer and creator of your own definition of a RichLife. And best of all, you don't have to wait to get started.

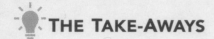

THE TAKE-AWAYS

- We all have a purpose here on earth. We all have God-given talents and gifts and an innate desire to explore them. Following this will lead us to discover our life purpose.

- The best way to serve others and humanity is by discovering and living out your life purpose.

- Once you have identified your giftings and talents, the most direct way to insure success is to use them in the service of others.

- Designing your ideal future and RichLife begins with identifying *who, what, when, where* and *why*.

- Listing how much and by when for your goals and objectives will advance you toward your RichLife every day.

ACTION STEPS

You've just finished reading a chapter devoted to the subject of life clarity. Congratulations. But you're not done yet. Reading this chapter won't take you as far down the path to your RichLife as *doing* the chapter. Take a few moments out of your busy day and complete the exercises scattered throughout the chapter, or, if you'd rather not mark up your book, join the RichLife family online and download the free *RichLife 10 Investments Action Guide* at www .RichLifeActionGuide.com. The *Action Guide* includes all the action exercises at the end of each chapter as well as the exercises outlined throughout the book. Joining the RichLife family will also give you access to additional actionable worksheets, workshops, workbooks, and a community of like-minded friends. Yes, that sounds like a lot of work, but they say it takes more muscles to frown than to smile.

These action steps are not only fun to do but self-revealing. In fact, you might even find yourself smiling while you do them.

- **Follow the clue to your purpose:** List five things you are passionate about. List the times in your life when you were the happiest and experienced the highest level of fulfillment. List five skills and talents that you feel are innately yours. List your top five values. Make a list of the people and professionals who you think could benefit from your skills.

- **Being enough, doing enough, having enough**: How does what you think about yourself affect what you are willing to try? Who are the people or circumstances that you think are preventing you from doing what you want? What is currently missing from your life that may be preventing you from doing what you would love to do?

- **Design your RichLife**: Identify the following seven things:

- Who are the people you want to spend time with?

- What gives you joy and satisfaction?

- What do you want to be doing on a daily basis?

- Why is this important to you?

- When, or what time of day, do you best perform?

- Where do you want to live and work?

- What is your definition of a RichLife?

- **Don't forget! Do it now!** Download your free copy of the *Action Guide* for *The RichLife: Ten Investments for True Wealth* at www.RichLifeActionGuide.com.

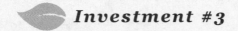 *Investment #3*

VIEW LIFE AS A SCHOOL

"As a progressive and evolving being, man is
where he is that he may learn that he may grow;
and as he learns the spiritual lesson which any
circumstance contains for him, it passes away
and gives place to other circumstances."
—JAMES ALLEN, author of *As a Man Thinketh*

WHEN THE BAD BECOMES GOOD

When something bad happens or doesn't go our way, it's easy to
convince ourselves that the world is out to get us, that some things
just aren't meant to be, or that we have horrible bad luck. Take this
to heart and you become defeated before you've even tried. This
way of thinking is a recipe for staying stuck, especially with regard
to our life purpose. It leads to repeating the same unhealthy choices
all the while hoping for a different outcome. This is one definition of insanity, and at one time or another we've all been guilty
of this kind of behavior. Albert Einstein once wrote that the most

important decision anyone ever makes is whether or not to view the universe as a friendly place. Let's take a closer look at this. Ask yourself, how do you view this experience called life? When something doesn't go as planned, how do you react? Are you the victim? Is life out to get you? Or are there lessons to be learned?

When it comes to our beliefs about life, there are those we have chosen and those we have been given. As an adult, sooner or later the time comes when it is necessary to re-evaluate those beliefs. You want to make conscious choices. Ask yourself whether or not a belief is helpful, whether or not it serves you. At the beginning of this book, I asked that you not only be open to new ways of looking at wealth, but that you also be willing to release those beliefs that are no longer helpful. In this chapter, I offer you a new way of looking at the "bad" things that happen in your life. I want to talk about viewing life as a school.

Anybody can choose to view life as a school, regardless of where they happen to live. Maggie Munyua in Nairobi, Kenya talks about life school as part of her journey to achieving a RichLife. She shares the following opinion:

> The many things we know now are the things we have learned while at life school. The discoveries we have made in our lives we have made while at this school. Without it, you cannot learn. My true story in life as a school is real. Without having gone through this school, I wouldn't be where I am today.

A BEAUTIFUL SURPRISE

Ten years ago in the capitol city of Nairobi, Maggie landed a contract deal to publish a book in Kenya for the African market. Maggie saw this project as a great opportunity and didn't verify the fine print of the contract. When the author flew to Kenya and made the 50 percent down payment toward the project, the publishing began, but that was all Maggie ever saw of the author. It was also all she ever saw in the way of funding for the project.

A few weeks later, Maggie found herself at the printers with 20,000 copies of a book and a huge balance to pay. She tried to track the author down, but he had changed his phones, left the country, and changed his address. There was no way to trace him, and Maggie was left in a bad situation. She had to work smart to avoid ending up in court with the printers and tarnishing her image.

This is where the story gets interesting. Anybody who has ever taken a chance on their dream can relate to Maggie's predicament. She had a large debt, 20,000 books, and a contract that named her responsible. At this point, Maggie could have chosen to react in any number of ways. What she chose to do was to face her responsibilities and take ownership of the problem. She negotiated with the printers to get the 20,000 copies paid for, and then she set about learning what she could about book distribution and marketing.

One Sunday afternoon while sitting outside her house, an idea to market the book through social media and email came to her. Maggie got out her laptop and got to work. That night, she went to sleep pretty exhausted. The following morning, she awoke to find her email inbox flooded with book orders from all over Africa. These orders were the most beautiful surprise.

Maggie headed straight to the printers with real orders that needed to be filled. She distributed the books, got paid, and paid the printers in return. She also paid herself from the surplus of the sales.

This experience opened up a new avenue in Maggie's life, one that she hadn't thought of before. The experience showed her that people are out there looking for information, and it clarified her life purpose: to be the person to give that information in the form of books, magazines, or manuals. Life school demonstrated to Maggie that with every idea comes a journey and a destination that can yield results if you apply yourself to the curriculum. Maggie explains in her own words:

> Life school taught me that I don't have to be stuck at one point and do things over and over again and expect different results. I must do things differently for different results. In this lesson, I found my desire to be a publisher and opened up another avenue to become a distributor through a book caravan theme in Africa. Life is a school in my life.

LESSONS TO LEARN: WELCOME TO LIFE SCHOOL

In my own work as a financial professional, I began to see my life and success improve dramatically when I started viewing life more like a school as opposed to a battlefield, a trap, or a chess match. Viewing life as a school means that the "bad" things that happen are no longer a punishment. Instead, these events are lessons that take me to the next "grade level." This has become a very productive way to view failure. Like Maggie with her book contract, when something doesn't go the way I expected or hoped, I am able to look at the experience as a road marker, or a sign, alerting me to areas that need my attention. Sometimes they are directing me toward a different path altogether. By viewing life this way, failure is no longer "bad" but friendly. Let's take a closer look at the value of this model.

We all understand the basic concept of school and how it is built in a natural progression. In college you enroll in a degree or certificate program in your field of choice. First you enlist in a core curriculum of general studies that must be passed in order to advance to the classes in your major. Within that core curriculum, there are certain classes, which have many levels to them, that require prerequisites before advancement is possible. For example, Literature 101 and 102 must be completed before moving on to the

200 and 300 level classes. If you don't pass a required course, you have to take it again until you get the passing grade.

A mentor and dear friend, Steve D'Annunzio, shared this concept of "life as a school" with me and as I said before, applying it has greatly improved my life. He pointed out that our time here on earth can be viewed as time in school. There are lessons we must learn to move forward, and when we haven't learned them we need to repeat the class over and over until we do. The sticking point here is that each time a lesson is repeated, it becomes more painful.

Think about this concept in terms of your own life. Have you found yourself in the same bad relationship time and time again? Does it seem that you are repeatedly attracting the type of person who is wrong for you? Each time a relationship ends, does it become more painful?

Maybe for you it's a pattern around money. You pay off your credit cards, swearing to never use them again, only to find yourself in debt over your head just a year later. Maybe you have a tendency to fall for the "high risk/high gain" promise. It looks good at the outset, and yet time and again, it turns against you and goes south almost before you know what hit you. You're sure next time will be different. And so you try again. But it never is different and each time you have even more to lose.

If you're like some people, your repeated life lessons lie in your professional world. Moving from job to job, you are actively trying to improve your life, yet you run into the same problems in each place. The grass is always greener until you get there and realize it's the same stuff all over again. The names and faces have changed, but the situation is exactly the same. Does that sound familiar?

In each of these scenarios, there is a strong possibility that the lessons contained here have yet to be learned. In fact, they probably offer exactly what you need to learn in order to move to the next step and achieve exactly what you want.

This model is very helpful as it applies to the area of our life purpose. If you have repeatedly experienced failure at the kind of work you wish to do, then maybe it's time to stop and ask yourself what the lesson is. If you view life as a school and accept failure as a guide, you'll be well on your way to success.

Karen Armstrong *did* fail in the convent, and when she examined that a new direction was revealed to her. Maggie Munyua nearly failed as a book publisher, which led her to success in marketing and a new career path as a book distributor. Back in the days when I was running through clients to meet my goal in numbers, I had to admit to a certain degree of failure. I was no longer satisfied with my work or my level of performance. To admit that something *isn't* working is one of the most productive things that you can do. To take that a step further and ask yourself *why* it isn't working can and will lead to advancement.

With regard to life school, here is the secret you need to know: If you don't pass a required course, you will have to take it again until you get the passing grade. This is why the same things keep popping up. No one is out to "get you," and it's not "bad luck." Regardless of what area the lesson is in, it *will* keep popping up until you finally "get it."

WAKE-UP CALL

Justin had a gift for teaching. His family said that "Justin could teach a fish how to wear pants," and it was assumed he would go on to someday become a beloved professor. Only Justin had his own ideas. Being a teacher didn't sound all that exciting to him, and besides, he had a fear. While he was fine one on one or in a small group setting, speaking in front of large groups absolutely terrified him.

He never got over this fear. He took a class in public speaking, but that only confirmed his ineptitude. The idea of giving lectures or speeches of any kind was simply out of the question, and so Justin shut down a part of himself and went in a different direction altogether. Following in the footsteps of his best friend, Justin became a pilot with a major commercial airline. He enjoyed the excitement of flying and the way he looked in his pilot's uniform. He attracted a lovely girl whom he went on to marry, and his family enjoyed all the benefits that being a pilot allowed. But then in the spring of 2001, something unexpected happened. Life gave him a wake-up call.

After a series of dramatic episodes, Justin's two-year-old daughter was diagnosed with severe Autism Spectrum Disorder (ASD). The news was devastating to the new father. The family experienced an emotional year compounded by lack of knowledge and constant sleep deprivation. In the middle of this, new flight regulations brought on by the events of 9/11 made work more complicated. Justin's career took a nose dive. Due to extreme sleep deprivation, Justin made an oversight that resulted in a lawsuit. When his case was brought before the board, things didn't go well. He was disqualified from receiving an FAA Airmen Medical Certificate required to act as "Pilot-in-Command" and Justin was grounded.

It seemed as if his entire world had fallen apart. But he still had his family. Following the old leanings of his heart, Justin pursued knowledge as a balm for his wounds. He wanted more than anything to help his daughter, but he knew nothing about ASD. Learning about her disorder consumed him. He read incessantly and pursued a degree in special education with a Master's specializing in ASD. It was a tight couple of years, but Justin was driven, and with the help of a student loan he and his wife got through it together.

Because of the rising number of children being diagnosed with ASD, Justin had no problem getting hired in the school district of his choice. He now has a unique classroom that looks like no other in the school. Using the latest research findings and therapies,

Justin works with a small and select group of kids to help transform young lives. His work is recognized by other teachers, the principal, and of course the parents. He has received numerous awards and promotions. Parents come to him with their fears and their hopes, and he is able to speak to them as only a parent who has been there can. He loves his job, and excels at it in a way nobody else could.

Sometimes life is painful. Sometimes things happen that are hard to accept. But within every circumstance lies a hidden lesson. Through a series of negative events, Justin learned that he was a teacher. Within every hardship lies the chance for growth. If the lesson can be found, then the bad can be turned around. It can become a gift.

COMPARING CURRICULUMS

Often when it comes to our life calling, many of us don't answer the first time around. We have our own reasons, just like Justin did, and we get off track. We find ourselves in places we never intended to be. But if we are paying attention, if we have the courage to view life as a school, we will find that its curriculum will serve to uncover our purpose.

Life provides us with the exact curriculum we need and the lessons we learn, however painful, provide the wisdom needed in order to find this purpose.

Justin is able to offer valuable help to parents and their children in the ASD spectrum only because of the wisdom he gained by experiencing it himself. It seems unfair. Who would wish this for their child? We must keep in mind that we don't get to choose the curriculum, and everyone's is different. Even those people who at a glance seem to have it "easy" have done the hard work required of life's school. Justin turned things around for himself by choosing to look at what *he* could do with the situation at hand. Everyone has a row to hoe and we all have a story. I've had clients who have experienced the painful loss of a loved one and asked the question, "How is this a good thing?" Well, it's not a good thing. And my heart goes out to them. But what I have seen is that the most powerful purposes often come from going through life's most difficult curriculums. So if life's been tough, you may very well be on your way to a Ph.D. in life school.

Answer the call, and you'll discover the purpose. These are the people who become most valuable to society because of the wisdom they have to offer. These are the people who can teach us the most as we work through our own curriculum.

We don't get to choose what will happen. But we always have a choice as to how we are going to respond. By choosing to gain wisdom, we are able to offer a greater gift to the world.

FROM THE BUMPS TO THE SLAPS

Sometimes life school has a real sense of humor. If you're paying attention, you will find that daily reminders show up constantly, just when you need them. Next time something as simple as a bump on the head happens, ask yourself, what was I thinking about? Chances are your mind was on a negative tangent, and the bump came as a reminder. Looking for these little lessons on a daily basis can go a long way to helping you become a better steward of both your energy and time.

Irene and her husband were on a tight retirement budget until the new Medicare laws came into effect. Because of her husband's medication needs, it threw everything in a tumult, and Irene was left with a swamp of red tape and paper work. She went to a professional seeking advice, but he didn't understand their situation correctly and botched things up. After trying for a second time to get help with yet again no results, Irene took a different route. "It felt like I kept getting my hand slapped," she said, "so I stopped reaching and started learning." It took her a full year to get it all sorted out, but now no one knows more about Medicare laws than Irene. She and her husband started an online business to help their fellow senior citizens learn what they need to know about their Medicare benefits. They have discovered a whole new career that they love, while in their seventies. Because of their ordeal, things are much more comfortable for them now. They have another income stream and together have become valuable, vibrant members of their community

As we endeavor to discover our life purpose and design our RichLife, it's important to be mindful of those life lessons that lead us to exactly the place we need to be at just the right moment. When something goes wrong, regardless of how small or irritating, ask yourself if it might not be a wake-up call. Time to stop, listen, and learn. It might be an opportunity to reevaluate who you are and what you are doing. If you can invest in the idea of life as a school, you will find that there are no mistakes, only necessary and valuable lessons. You can enjoy the times that are great and realize that when times are not so great, you must be in the midst of a lesson that contains exactly what is needed to take you to the next level. Often these next levels are places you never thought you could go. Places that exceed your own highest expectations. As Jerry Garcia once said, "Once in a while you get shown the light in the strangest of places if you look at it right." Viewing life as a school can help you find that light.

PORTFOLIO BUILDER

We can begin investing in *Life 101* right away. Viewing life as a school means you don't have to get stuck learning the same lessons over and over and over. As a wise steward of your energy, don't waste time by assigning blame. Instead, take responsibility and look for the lesson in things both big and small, and you'll find yourself moving closer to your RichLife.

THE TAKE-AWAYS

I would like to share a great reminder that I have posted in my office. I read it often so that I can be reminded that I am in a school called *life*. And in this wonderful school even the bad is good. Make a copy for yourself, hang it on the wall, post it near your desk, or tape it inside your locker. Feel free to share this reminder with others.

1. We live in a school called Life.

2. There are no mistakes, only valuable lessons.

3. A lesson will be repeated until it is learned.

4. Each time a lesson is repeated it becomes more painful.

 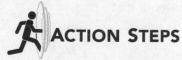

The greatest lesson we can learn is to choose Love over Fear.

ACTION STEPS

One of the most valuable things you can do in the life school curriculum is to create a life school journal. This journal doesn't necessarily have to be in written form. It can be a drawing journal, a series of spoken recordings, or prayerful meditations done at the end of the day. The most important thing to establish with the life school journal is the habit of looking for the lesson.

- **Step #1:** At the end of each day, take five minutes to acknowledge what went right. Think about what happened during the day that you were grateful for, big or small. It can be the smile from your daughter, the acknowledgement from your boss, or the step in the right direction, no matter how small. Gratitude is a key component of inner happiness, wellbeing, and a sense of self-worth. (For more exercises designed to help you practice daily gratitude habits, see Chapter One of the *RoadMap to a RichLife* workbook.)

- **Step #2:** After you have recognized the good, take five minutes to acknowledge what happened during the day that didn't go the way you wanted or would have liked. It can also be valuable to take a step back while in the midst of a particularly stressful problem or dilemma, especially at work. This step is simply about identifying what went wrong. It is not about "the who" or "the why." Avoid feelings of blame, shame, or judgment. Your job is to simply acknowledge what didn't go the way you hoped.

- **Step #3:** Look closely at the problem, dilemma or situation, and ask yourself, what is the lesson here? What can I learn from this experience? Try to avoid finger-pointing and blame. Instead, seek a proactive approach. For example, instead of saying, "I have learned never to trust anybody every again," say, "I have learned that I need to educate myself in this particular area."

- **Bonus Step:** Download your free copy of the Action Guide for *The RichLife: Ten Investments for True Wealth* at www.RichLifeActionGuide.com.

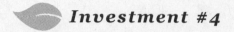 *Investment #4*

CULTIVATE MEANINGFUL RELATIONSHIPS

"Shared joy is a double joy; shared
sorrow is half a sorrow."
—Swedish Proverb

Of all the chapters in the book, this one speaks to a point we can most readily agree upon. Most people understand the value of a mother and father, the value of a friend. If we are a parent or guardian ourselves, then we have experienced the love of a child and know what a profound bond that is. If we have been lucky enough to find someone to share our lives with, then we understand the value of having a person who loves us through thick and thin, in sickness and in health. Yet out of all our relationships, these people closest to us are often the ones we take most for granted.

WHO WOULD I BE WITHOUT YOU?

When was the last time you looked at the person you see every day—your wife, your partner, your husband, mother, brother, or son—and acknowledged them for the support they have given you? Think about it. What would you say? "If it wasn't for you, I would not have been able to accomplish _____."

So often we hear negative stories about married life. We all joke around about the "old ball and chain," and we act like getting married means the end of life as we know it. A partnership between two people doesn't have to be that way. Just as two sticks placed side by side are harder to break than a single stick alone, people can also become stronger when aligned with another. When two people are in a committed and supportive relationship, they are able to accomplish great things, things they wouldn't have been able to accomplish alone. In a 2013 interview with *The Atlantic*, bestselling author Stephen King reveals one of his secrets to success: "I stayed married." You can get more done when in a healthy, stable relationship than when going it all alone.

Relationship educator and author Yudy Cid puts it this way: "Marriage doesn't just mean, *you must stand here with me*. It's about the power of being part of a team. The power that comes from saying, *I will stand here for you*." As host of the bilingual program *Vida en Alto* and a pioneer in the marriage education movement for the Latino community of New York City, Yudy teaches that it's *not* the issues that drive people apart. *The happy couple and the stressed couple both have the same issues*. It's the way you handle the conflict that makes the difference. Will you stand there for your partner? Will they stand there for you?

STAND BY ME

Roberto and Julia lived together in a one bedroom apartment in New York City. Their daughter, Anna, slept on a sofa bed in the middle of the living room, and their bills were paid by the income earned by Roberto. During the day, Roberto worked construction; four nights a week he drove a taxi. Roberto and Julia were living off one income because they had a plan. The money from Roberto's two jobs was used to pay the bills, put food on the table, and provide for Anna's day care while Julia went to college to earn her degree.

It took them four years, but together they stayed the course. Roberto's friends teased him for going home every night after work instead of out for drinks, but Roberto didn't let it bother him. His father scolded him for spending his money on childcare when his wife didn't have a job, but Roberto told him, "Anna has to study. Building a dream takes more than just commitment. It takes resources." At the end of the day, Roberto came home to his small apartment and ate a simple meal of beans and rice with his family. He read a book to his daughter and then kissed his wife and daughter goodnight before heading out for the night shift, driving his taxi.

Meanwhile Julia went to her classes. Sometimes she feared she wouldn't graduate. She would come home after a frustrating day of classes, a day when all the other students seemed younger and smarter, and she would tell Roberto, "I can't do this. I'm not smart enough. I'm too old to start a new career, and you're working too hard!" And Roberto would look her in the eye and tell her, "You are going to be a great teacher. I know you, and I know you can do this."

It took them time, but those four years would have gone by anyway, whether or not they had the plan. Because they stood by each other, Julia graduated from college and received her degree. Then came the day when she got her first job, teaching second grade at an elementary school. Everyone in the family shared in the success of this accomplishment. Roberto and Julia are now enjoying the American Dream. Because of Julia's teaching job, they have benefits and health insurance and the privilege of maternity leave. Julia was able to have another child, and they bought a three-bedroom house in a better neighborhood. As a teacher, Julia's schedule is in flow with the schedule of her children, and Roberto doesn't have the additional stress of worrying about picking up or dropping off the kids. He also no longer has the financial pressure of having to work two jobs.

Although it was Julia who got the degree, everybody in the family got the benefit. The benefit of Julia's education was an investment that will continue to provide for this family for the rest of their lives. But she did not do it alone. Julia and her husband were a team, and because of that they now have a much better life.

A POINTED QUESTION

Roberto and Julia's story is a powerful example of what can be accomplished when we have the support of good people in our lives. Unfortunately, it also happens that the people who support us the most are the ones we take for granted the most. These are the people who have always been there for us, and so we just assume they always will be. Sometimes, we treat them poorly without even meaning to. We even forget to be kind.

I want to share with you a little exercise that I often do when I hold a *Keys to a RichLife* seminar. I ask this very pointed question:

 If you had great health and enjoyed all the normal physical capabilities, and yet you knew you had exactly six months to live—what would you do?

I then make the challenge even more difficult by allowing only *sixty seconds* for all the attendees to write down at least *five* things.

It's an interesting thing to watch as the faces grow serious and intent. The room becomes hushed, and all I hear are the scribbles of pens furiously writing answers.

I don't think it's any secret what most of the answers are. I've never once had anyone write down that they would immediately go out and buy a bigger house. Or invest in more stocks. Or ask for a promotion at work.

People almost always write down something that has to do with the people in their lives. With the relationships most important to them—a spouse or partner, children, parents, siblings, perhaps even a long-lost friend. When faced with a short-term ultimatum, most people want to spend time investing in relationships, not things. They want to invest in those human assets that don't come with a price tag, and as such, these are often the very relationships most easily taken for granted.

I finish off the exercise by coming back with the pointed follow-up question: Why wait for a death sentence in order to spend time with those you care about the most? Why not start now?

It's a sobering question; one that causes many people to stop and reassess how they currently invest their time on a day-to-day basis.

This is especially true for *driven* personality types who are so goal focused that anything not in line with those goals is pushed to the side. Oftentimes these "things" are the people they live with, the people and relationships in their daily lives. Spouses are no longer number one, but number two or number three on the list. The family that they rationalize "doing it all for" are seen less and less. As the goals expand and become more ambitious, these relationships get knocked farther and farther down the priority pole, and as a result family grows distant, friendships erode, and bonds of trust are often damaged past the point of repair. When the *goal* has finally been reached, the very people it was all for are gone or past the point of caring

This was the state of things when I first met with the client, Richard, who I have come to think of as the "Miserable Multimillionaire." His two sons had grown up never really knowing who their father was and, as a result, felt bitter and rejected. He didn't know who they were, either, yet in my client's mind everything he had done was for them and their mother. He wanted them to have the best that money could buy. This is the great irony that I see happen so often, when the very people the goals were for end up lost to those who achieved them. But by the time I appeared on the scene, this family not only lived in separate homes but in separate states, only speaking to one other on the holidays, if that.

It was never this father's intention to estrange his sons. He never meant to cause so much pain for the woman he married. There have been instances after my seminars where an individual has left and gone on to mend a broken relationship. It's pretty exciting to hear that feedback. When they take the time to make that phone call, apologize to a sibling, sit with an elderly parent, they get closer to their own happiness. Really this chapter is a reminder of what we all know to be true already: time invested in people is never lost. The return on this investment pays high dividends, and the earnings are incalculable, even if presented in the form of a hard lesson learned.

DO IT TODAY

The best memories I have of my dad are not of the big trips we took or any of the stuff he got me. What stands out most in my mind are the years between the ages of five and twelve when he coached my little league football team. He was a busy man with his own business to manage, yet somehow he made time for football. As a kid, I never stopped to ask myself *how* he made the time, but he was always there to coach me. The things he taught me out on that field and the small victories we shared together added up to some of the most meaningful moments in my life. It's how I remember my dad.

My friend Carol remembers the weekends her dad took the family out hiking. He was a career military man and often gone for months at a time on deployment, but when he was home, weekends were for family. Wherever they happened to be living, they explored the state parks, learned about famous battles, and took to the trails. He taught her how to track, sometimes going off the path and leaving clues for her to follow. She and her siblings would have to figure out how to read those clues in an elaborate tracking game of "hide and seek." These are her favorite memories of her dad.

As a child, you take times like these for granted. It seems natural and right that an adult be there. But as a working parent living her own busy life, Carol wonders how her father did it, given the number of things always needing to be done on the weekends. Coaching a team is also a huge investment of time and energy, yet every season for eight years, my dad was there, investing between six and eight hours a week. It becomes clear that time for football and hiking isn't a given. It's a choice. You have to make the decision to invest in moments with your children and loved ones or they just don't happen. Those hours must be set aside, worked into your schedule. Spending time with people has to be planned for.

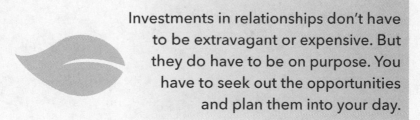

Investments in relationships don't have to be extravagant or expensive. But they do have to be on purpose. You have to seek out the opportunities and plan them into your day.

The truth is life *really is* that short. No one has the promise of tomorrow. I've seen it happen time and again with my clients who unexpectedly lost a loved one. My own father passed away when I was only twenty-three, making all those hours he invested in me even more valuable. Who are the people who have invested in you?

Who would you be without their love and support? And who are the people who deserve your time now?

For some people, it helps to have a set time and date that occurs regularly, such as a lesson, class, or coaching time. Remember Roberto and Julia in our earlier story? During the four years when Roberto worked nights, Julia would get up at 4 a.m. on those Saturday mornings to sit with Roberto when he came home from his late shift. She would fix him a meal and the couple would talk to one another, because Roberto didn't have to be at the construction site on Saturday mornings. Whether you set aside a day of the week or just a few hours, start out small—a meal together, a tennis game, a ten-minute phone call. The point is to *be* with that person, sit with them, listen to them, find out what they are up to. Nothing more than that is required. A walk after dinner, a drive to get ice cream, a cup of coffee with a friend—schedule it in. Relationships must be invested in *today,* not put off until tomorrow.

THE "WHEN I, THEN I..." GAME

One thing I hear a lot of in regard to making time for others is what I affectionately call the *when I, then I* game. It's one I hear a lot of, especially with regard to *retirement*.

- "When I retire, then I can make time for the grandkids."

- "When I retire, then I can spend more time with my spouse."

- "When I retire, then I can finally join that bowling league."

With younger couples, the *when I then I* game usually goes something like:

- "When I finish remodeling the basement, then I can take my spouse out to dinner."

- "When I'm done with this big job, then I can go out again with my friends."

- "When I get that promotion, then I'll take my kids to that great amusement park."

The problem with this kind of thinking is that it leads to a bankrupt relationship account.

Because you are waiting for some future event, you aren't investing in these relationships *now*. Meanwhile, you are constantly drawing on these people every day because they are the ones on whom you rely in so many little ways. It's easy to forget that those withdrawals add up. These accounts need to be replenished; something needs to be flowing back to them *now*, not when all your wishes and dreams come true. We have to remember that generosity is a function of the heart, not of the wallet. *You make the time now with whatever amount of time you have.* Waiting for the ideal time, the ideal amount of money, the ideal circumstance is the exact same thing as not doing it at all. Waiting until you retire, playing the *when I, then I* game, results in relationships that become taxed, overdrawn, and maxed out. You finally get around to them, and you find that the account is closed, and they are no longer there.

DON'T SPILL THE OIL

There is a wonderful parable told in the book *The Alchemist* by Paulo Coelho that speaks well to the value of relationships. A young boy is asked to carry a spoonful of precious oil while taking a tour of a grand and beautiful castle. He is told not to spill so much as one drop, and so he walks around the castle with his eyes on the spoon. When he returns from his tour, he is scolded for missing out on the experience of his surroundings and is sent back out again. This time, the boy takes in everything—the gardens, the tapestries, even the pastries in the kitchen. What marvels, what delights! But when he returns, alas, he finds all the oil spilled from his spoon.

This idea reveals the secret to happiness: you want to enjoy all the riches that life has to offer without spilling any oil from your spoon.

That precious oil represents the most valuable of assets in our life—human assets. These are the people we care about, the people in our everyday life, and it includes our own health and wellbeing. The goals we set and the exciting journeys we take must be performed in balance with the stewardship of our human assets, just as the boy balanced the spoon. We must take care to often check the drops of oil to keep those relationships intact and nourished, to keep our own bodies rested and replenished. This goes back to our earlier discussion of money. Just as the accumulation of bank notes must never be given priority over the people it was meant to serve, so too our life goals must not come at the cost of our human assets.

It has often been said that success must be measured against what was given up in order to attain it. If you find that you are being asked to give up everything, including the oil in your spoon, it might be time to make a different choice. Find the balance between personal achievement and human relationships, and you will discover the secret to a happy and fulfilled life.

INVEST IN PEOPLE

Outside the family circle, there are many other friends and acquaintances with whom you have relationships. These can be business colleagues or the neighbor who takes care of your mail when you are out of town. How well are you cultivating those important friendships? The people I meet who are the most fulfilled are those who have taken time to invest in all the relationships in their life, not just the big ones. And while it might sound like an exhausting thing to undertake, the converse is actually true given the nature of the investment.

With regard to cultivating meaningful relationships, here is the secret: Everything you give to others only comes back to you. Good or bad, ugly or inspired, every kindness is multiplied, every neglect compounded. This is especially obvious when it comes to our children. The famous hit song from 1974, "Cat's in the Cradle" by Harry Chapin, points to this when he writes about the father who never had time for his son. It was based on the real life story of a politician and the boy who kept hoping, always responding with, "But we'll get together then, Dad. You know we'll have a good time then." The *then* never came, and when the father finally got around to it, his son was all grown and it was he who had no time for the father.

And as I hung up the phone, it occurred to me,
He'd grown up just like me.
My boy was just like me.

It is especially helpful to remember that we teach our children by what we do, not by what we say. So, too, in our relationships with others, we show them how we want to be treated by the way in which we treat them. This is why everything we do comes back to us, and why investments in relationships are the best investments we could ever make. The standard golden rule definitely applies here, and as illustrated by "Cat's in the Cradle," what *isn't* done will also, in turn, *not* be done unto you. When you need to talk to someone, no one will be willing to drop what they are doing. When you've had a hard won success, no one will be around to share your joy. This takes all the juice out of life and dampens all the fun. Building relationships is a purposeful thing. What you do today is remembered far more than the empty promise of *We'll do it tomorrow.*

Investing in relationships is definitely a two-way street. The more you invest, the more you get back and the richer your life becomes. There is nothing sadder than seeing clients who meet every financial goal they set for themselves but end up losing their family. These people end up in bad shape. Conversely, the clients who come to me with their finances in ruin but good people by their side, well, they end up being okay. They end up making it. I learned a long time ago that there's nothing you can't do if you have enough friends by your side. The value of relationships cannot, in my opinion, be underestimated. What you put into them comes back, and the good comes back in ways more bountiful than you ever imagined.

NETWORKING WITH INTENTION

If you find a twenty-dollar bill on the street, this is a bit of grace. You can invest that in something meaningful, or you can let it get lost in the jumble of your pocket, meaning to think about what to do with it later. The same is also true of relationships. The people who show up in our lives are like gifts, arriving at the perfect time. You will never know of their value until you take the time to get to know them, to nurture the relationship. This can mean spending as little as a minute to hear about someone's day, or taking the time to have lunch with someone. This certain individual may be the very person who will introduce you to a future spouse, help you with a critical business deal, or turn into a cherished lifetime friend. But you won't get any of that unless you give them your attention first

The common definition of networking—establishing relationships that refer business back to you by word of mouth—is one most of us are familiar with. However, most people don't realize that the same good tenets that apply to personal relationships also apply to the business world. Investing in business relationships this way is what I call *networking with intention*. If you approach these relationships with the same principles of good stewardship that we have been talking about for family and friends, aware of what you are investing in and why, success and growth is almost always assured.

With regard to developing new relationships and networking with intention, here is the secret that you need to know: always operate in the best interests of all involved.

This means that if it is bad for them, it is bad for you. On the home front, the same thing applies. You can apply this to your relationships with your spouse, your children, your friends. If staying late at the office to finish something up will cause suffering for your spouse, don't do it; come home and go in early the next day. If you are in a bad relationship, an amicable separation will give both of you the freedom to find something better. If rushing a job to get it done by deadline will greatly compromise the final product, give the client a call and find out what can be done. Nine times out of ten, a different delivery date will be more convenient for them, too.

What you are always seeking is a win/win situation, because those will produce the best results for everyone, every time. Keep in mind this basic secret, begin applying it to all your relationships, and positive results will occur. This principle goes back to the idea of being good stewards of our assets.

To nurture relationships requires a level of caring and the skill of listening. It requires that you be present, as with the boy and his teaspoon of oil. You watch over them, notice what they are doing and what you are doing. I like to ask what I call "feel good" questions. I try to get to know a person well enough to be able to inquire about something they care about. That could be anything from their latest fishing trip, to the grandchildren, to their hobbies. This kind of investment pays big dividends over the long term because you are then able to share in their joys and accomplishments. You get to be included in their inner circle, in the rich web of their lives. You get invited places, you get to see and do things you would have never before considered. It adds to your RichLife. And it only keeps getting better.

However, there are only so many hours in a day. It is certainly not your goal to be included in *everyone's* inner circle just as you wouldn't want *everyone* in yours. Investing in relationships is a selective process, one that needs to be done with attention and care. Just as I asked you earlier to examine your beliefs and discard those which are no longer helpful, it might be time to do the same with regard to your relationships.

TOXIC RELATIONSHIPS

Carl Jung once said that everything we find irritating about others can lead us to a better understanding of ourselves. We all have those people in our lives whose role at first might seem unclear. There are those who show up for certain periods in our lives, teaching us certain lessons, and then they move on or we move on. Some of the people in my life whom I thought would always be there aren't. And I am always surprised by the quality of the new relationships that continue to show up and enrich my life. Still there is another type of person—the one who keeps showing up to aggravate or make you miserable. Oftentimes, you can't seem to get rid of them. But take heart. Even these relationships are worth your attention because they, too, have a lesson to teach. They show us who we *do not* want to become, and they teach us how to set boundaries.

In my seminars, I talk about toxic relationships. These are the people who drain energy instead of give. These are the people into whose relationship accounts you are constantly making deposits without ever making withdrawals. Nothing good comes back. You leave them feeling drained, frazzled, and anxious about a new list of worries. Even talking with them on the phone can get you worked up. Sometimes, these relationships are so toxic, even *thinking* about them sends you down a road of negativity.

Being aware of our human assets calls us to become better stewards of our energy. Spending time with people who zap our precious energy is like making the choice to go into a fun house while trying to balance our spoon of precious oil. It only taxes our own health and our own energy. While sometimes this is necessary, we must be aware of the costs when it is happening too often. The relationships you want to invest your time in are those that are positive, supportive, and encouraging. It's important to discern the difference. Oftentimes in my seminars, we end up laughing because people will say to me, "You're telling me not to spend time with my mother!" And it's true, of course, because many times the people who are the most toxic to us are those with whom we have long histories or grew up with. They say we don't get to choose our family, yet they are the people who are always there for us. We can't just "discard" them the way you can an old belief. However, you can learn from them, and you can set boundaries.

If you are experiencing strong negative feelings around someone close to you, it might be time to take a step back. If you have identified a relationship that for you, at this time in your life, is toxic, you do have a choice. You don't have to be a martyr by enduring their company. But by the same token, it probably isn't a good idea to announce to them, "You are toxic to me. I don't want to be around you anymore."

A friend of mine we'll call Carmen has a sister with whom she shares everything, including an apartment. "No one can make me happier or more miserable than my sister," she realized. Carmen decided it was time to get her own place. She moved into a different apartment complex a few blocks away, but the sister kept dropping by unannounced, showing up all hours to borrow clothes or talk about her day. "I love my sister and I totally enjoy her company," Carmen explains, "but I couldn't enjoy the freedom of having my own space. So I set up a boundary. I told her she was always welcome at my place, but she had to call first. If I was home, great, but if I didn't answer, leave a message, and we'll get together at another time. This went a long way toward giving us both a little bit of independence. In many ways, we have a stronger relationship."

Once you have identified a relationship that you find toxic, it might be time to set up some boundaries. This might be something you discuss with them, or it might be a personal choice that you make on your own. Perhaps you decide to limit your exposure to them for a few weeks or months. Maybe you cut back on your calls or emails; maybe you decide to limit your texting. The choice is yours. A lot of people forget that it doesn't have to be an all or nothing deal. On the other hand, cutting off communication altogether might be a good idea for the time being. You might think, "I can't just stop talking to my mother!" But you can. If you spend the majority of your time arguing together, this will be good for both of you, a win/win, and chances are it won't last forever. There are varying degrees of unhealthy relationships. We are all wired differently. It's okay if you don't resonate with everyone.

If the toxic relationship you've identified is a close family member, then taking a break to figure out what it is about them that really rubs you the wrong way can also go a long way toward your own personal development. As evidenced earlier, what you are really responding to is a habit or flaw inside of you being mirrored by that other person. Figuring out what it is about them you find so bothersome will point to what you are working on personally.

The greatest spiritual teachers have all agreed on this: if you want to find out how *advanced* you are or how much you have grown as a person, just spend a week with your family and you'll find out!

Investing in relationships is a lot like budgeting your money. If you need two hundred extra dollars a month, the first place to start is by looking at things you can trim away that might not be the best use of your funds. This is also true of our time and how we spend it on others. There very well may be people in your life—high school friends, for example—whom you have outgrown. It might be time to send them a blessing and simply move on. Use that extra night a week to throw a ball on the lawn with your son, take someone you've just met to a movie, or take a class and invest in your own education. When it comes to the people in our life, "spoiled" is what happens when something is left alone on a shelf, unattended. This is so often the case with the people we leave behind, at home, the people who really care about us. It is the exact opposite of what we need to do. Don't let that happen to the relationships most important to you.

 ## PORTFOLIO BUILDER

One who lives a fulfilled RichLife understands that the people who are closest to us must not be taken for granted. They know that time with others must be planned for, set aside, and worked in to every day much the same way we budget our money. And they know that spending time with others is something to begin doing now, as a function of the heart. Healthy relationships are one of the keys to living a RichLife.

 ## THE TAKE-AWAYS

Use these to begin uncovering the secret to happier, more fulfilled relationships in your life today.

- Waiting for the ideal time, the ideal amount of money, the ideal circumstance is the exact same thing as not investing in relationships at all.

- Everything you give to others comes back to you. What you don't give will be absent from your life.

- With regard to dealing with others, always operate in the best interests of all involved.

 **ACTION STEPS**

- List three current relationships that you would like to make an investment in today.

1. _____

2. _____

3. _____

- Pick a day and a time and make a plan to invest time with one of those people on your list. This can be as simple as taking a walk. It doesn't have to be extravagant. A lot of people make the mistake of putting it off because they think it has to be really special when really it only has to happen. Anything is better than not trying. As with our previous exercise, give yourself the goal of how much and by when

I plan to invest in my relationship with _____ by spending _____(amount of time) with them doing _____ beginning _____.

Example: I plan to invest in my relationship with Sam by spending one night a week with him as a friend, not talking about work or the kids, beginning this Saturday.

- Think of a relationship that is having a negative impact on your time and energy. What actions can be put into place that will improve the stewardship of your time and energy? List three things that you can begin doing now that will allow for some boundaries.

My relationship with _____ is currently hard on me and not in my best interest. Three things I can do now to set up boundaries are:

1. _____

2. _____

3. _____

Example: My relationship with my brother is currently hard on me and not in my best interest. Three things I can do now to set up boundaries are: I will stop arguing with my brother in emails and keep our communication limited to planning purposes such as birthdays or family get-togethers. I will take a break from posting and commenting on Facebook. I will talk to someone outside my family when I need advice.

- Think of one relationship that you think you may have outgrown. For example, maybe that Friday night poker group with your high school buddies no longer serves you. Maybe the time would be better spent in other ways, such as at a night class that will expand your life purpose. By streamlining your relationship investments, you will have more time freed up to invest in one of the new relationships identified above.

I feel I have outgrown my relationship with _____. I would rather be spending my time with _____ doing _____.

Example: I feel I have outgrown my relationship with Cecil. I would rather be spending time with myself doing work on my business plan.

- **Bonus Gift**: Find all of the above exercises by downloading your free copy of the Action Guide for *The RichLife: Ten Investments for True Wealth* at www.RichLifeActionGuide.com.

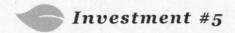 *Investment #5*

CREATING UNIQUE EXPERIENCES ON PURPOSE

"Be bold and courageous. When you look back on your life, you will regret the things you didn't do more than the things you've done."

—H. JACKSON BROWN, JR., author of
Life's Little Instruction Book

LIFE'S FIELD TRIPS

Do you remember as a kid how exciting it was to go on a class field trip? Going somewhere new, boarding the bus with all your friends, and then being transported to another world entirely? Any kind of a trip offered a welcome break from routine as well as inspiring ideas and career possibilities. And best of all, everything was planned out for you. All you had to do was show up with the bag lunch.

As an adult, it isn't very often that someone plans a field trip for you, yet even grown children benefit from such outings. You don't need a signed permission slip in order to give yourself an adventure. Unique experiences can be had alone or with others, with or without the purchase of a plane ticket, with or without weeks of planning. Life's field trips are experiences that we can give ourselves. They allow us to try a new thing, be it a different way home or a park we've never been to. These events happen out of the office, away from school, outside of the practical every day. They offer a break from ordinary routine, and this is why we remember them—because we are somewhere new, we adopt what I think of as *the traveler's mentality*. Our senses become sharpened; life becomes fresh again

Going back to our analogy of life school, in any classroom, regardless of how good the teacher, a student will forget up to 75 percent of the lesson the minute they leave the classroom. To have an experience with a living, breathing person as opposed to a textbook, however, secures the lesson permanently in the mind of a student. This is why educational field trips were designed, and the same kind of thing can be applied to our everyday life. *Experiences are what we remember*, which is why life school puts us through the wringer in an experiential way. It is the most effective way to teach a lesson. The good news here is that we also have the ability *to give ourselves* experiences that are *pleasant*. We have the ability, as adults, to design our own field trips, to create our own unique experiences.

These trips don't have to be extravagant, and I will go into that later. A simple outing at the beach has the potential to create a life memory just as easily as that wonderful trip to Greece. A field trip might not even be a real trip at all but a simple, deliberate departure from the everyday. They can be experiences you create intentionally for your own benefit as time alone doing something you love—a few stolen hours in the basement sewing room, a night on the roof with the telescope. It can be breakfast with the Little League® team or an outing to Appalachia State Park. Going to "that place" you always meant to go, visiting, exploring, experiencing. The Field Trip Directory, an online directory promoted by Family Publications LTD, states on its website, ClassTrips.com: "Though not every field trip is a life-changing event, these trips certainly have the potential to become lifelong memories." Anything we plan for ourselves, regardless of how small, has the potential to become a living gift. A memory we can turn over and over in our thoughts at any time we choose. A treasure of the mind. These experiences that we create for ourselves have the ability to add significantly to our RichLife. In fact, they become a greater part of our wealth, more so than you might think. More so than I ever thought.

THE GREATEST STORIES EVER TOLD

Warren and Izzy made an appointment to talk to me about their finances after Warren's mother passed away. They arrived together, he wearing a suit and a tie in the most vivid color he could find, and his wife in a bright hat and scarf, carrying a handbag to match. This was how Warren's mother liked to dress—in bold splashes of living color—and together they were honoring her memory as they sat down to manage her finances. She had left them a sum of money, and the subject of travel came up.

"Yes," Izzy replied, hands on her lap. "We would like to take a trip to New York City to see a live taping of the *David Letterman Show*." When she looked over at her husband, she smirked, and that started him shaking. It was a fit of giggles that overcame him, and once Izzy joined him, the laughing didn't stop. Together between the two of them they could hardly get the story out.

"My mom always wanted to see the Big Apple," Warren started, "but growing up we never went anywhere because Dad didn't want to sit in a metal coffin crammed with a bunch of strangers."

"And buses made his mom sick."

"Buses made her sick, and so did car trips, and so they never went anywhere. But then when I got this internship in New York City and Izzy and I were living in Brooklyn, Mom just decided to go. She booked her own flight. We had this tiny apartment and I was working two jobs and Izzy was still in school. We were both really busy but I was excited. I really wanted to plan something special for her."

On the day she was due to arrive, Warren was still racking his brain, trying to come up with an idea. Something they could do that would really give her a great experience of New York City.

"And then on the way to the Penn Station," Warren explains, "we passed the studio where they film the *David Letterman Show* and I thought, 'This is it! She loves David Letterman!' The marquee advertised a live show taping that night, and I figured since it wasn't even noon, if we got in line early, we could still get tickets.

"We rented a locker for her stuff," Izzy chimed in, "and took her right over to the theater. It was just past eleven-thirty in the morning and we were the first people in line. We were all so excited; I was playing hooky from my classes and Warren had called in sick or something. I think we made standing there look like a lot of fun. We both took turns running out to get Mom food or something to drink from the street carts. She was just so interested in everything and everybody. After a while this couple came up and asked us what we were doing."

"We're standing in line for tickets to the *David Letterman Show*!" Warren says. "And we're the first ones in line!"

"Really?" they asked, "Do they still have tickets?"

"Oh, I don't know," he said, "but I'll be the first in line to find out!"

Well, they figured that their chances were pretty good, also, being the number two couple in line, and so they joined the threesome outside under the marquee. After about an hour or so, the line got longer, and by about 4 o'clock, the anticipation had really begun to build up.

"There were maybe fifty or so people in line behind us," Warren says.

"At least fifty," corrected Izzy. "It was winding down the sidewalk."

Gradually the city lights came on and it started to cool off. Warren got his mom a cup of coffee and the people in line behind them started to grumble, wondering when they would finally be let in.

"Then at about five-thirty," Warren recalls, "I finally saw an usher walk past on the other side of the doors. I tapped on the glass and he saw us all out there. He got this look on his face and he came over and opened the door.

"'What are you all doing out here?' he asked in a low, concerned voice. I stepped up to the door.

"'Well I'm here to get tickets for tonight's show!'

"The usher looked at us all and then looked at me. 'We don't sell tickets here. We do that at the ticket door around the corner. And they sold out hours ago. Sorry.'

"Well, I turned around and looked at my wife and mother. And as the usher shut the door my mother mouths the words, *Get out of here, now!* She took both of us by our arms and we tore out of there, dashing down the street and into the first cab we saw, leaving behind all those people.

"'They're going to be mad as hell when they figure it out!' my mom said. And then she looked at my face and burst out laughing. And then we all started laughing, and we were laughing so hard that tears were pouring down our faces. We never did see the *David Letterman Show,* but I never laughed so much in my whole life as I did that night in the back of that cab. I'll never forget it."

THE VALUE OF EXPERIENCE

One of the most important lessons my clients have taught me is that regrets come not from the things that we try, but from the things we don't try. Even so-called failures have their value, as in the true story illustrated above. My clients don't look back on their experiences and regret what didn't go as planned. They don't see them as failures. In the spirit of Thomas Edison with his trials of the light bulb, it's not that he failed 10,000 times before getting it right; it's that he had 10,000 different experiences before finding the light bulb. Experience is the stuff of life. It's why we are here and what really adds to a person's wealth beyond the ordinary parameters of paper assets.

One of my own favorite *Relationship Investments* is visiting with retirees. I love to see the looks exchanged between couples who have been together for decades. Or the laughter that is shared between them before a story has even started because they both know it so well. Sometimes they step on each other's lines; sometimes they get a little choked up. They're so sure of the story, so sure they can tell it best without leaving anything out.

These meetings are just priceless to me, and when I realized that I stumbled on a revelation. After a meeting like the one described earlier with Warren and Izzy, I realized that those experiences they had shared were *still* being shared because they had become memories and as such, they had become an asset. An asset whose value can only be described as *priceless*.

Memories cannot be taxed, stolen, or lost in a lawsuit, nor do they depreciate over time. In fact, better yet, the more they are withdrawn and told over and over again, the better they get. There is no penalty, withdrawals can be made as early as the next day, and doing so only makes them stronger. What other asset can boast this kind of return?

I started asking my clients, after hearing a particularly funny or poignant story, "I bet you wouldn't trade that experience for all your net worth, would you?"

And the answer is always, without exception, the same.

"No we wouldn't," they say. "We wouldn't trade it for all the world."

With regard to investing in life experiences, here is the secret: Experiences shared or had alone become our memories, the most valuable assets that you can acquire.

PURPOSEFUL PLANNING: WRITE YOUR BUCKET LIST

We all have plans. Places we'd like to visit, things we'd like to do, and people who we'd like to do those things with. I like to think of this chapter as *the bucket list,* and in many ways it closely relates to the previous chapter on relationships. In the same way that relationships must be nurtured and planned for, so too must life's unique experiences. Adventures and happenings with those we love and care about seldom *just happen.* They have to be planned for, the time has to be set aside, and those plans have to be acted upon. For example: A date with your spouse, a family reunion, or a trip to the Egyptian pyramids. The list is endless and the plans can be big or small. Only you know what's on your list. But I ask you the question I often bring up in my seminars: have you written it down? What's on your bucket list? What are the things you want to do, the places you want to see, and the experiences you want to create with those you love?

Writing down your plans and putting the list in a place where you will see it every day is one step further toward their actualization. By creating a list, energy is added to the plans. The list gets read by you and by others. It gets talked about more than it would if it wasn't written down. Help comes along that would never have shown up otherwise. It keeps those plans active and alive, and pretty soon, step by step, they start to happen.

STARTING WITH THE SMALL

You may be saving and scrimping to take that long-dreamed-of vacation in Europe, but in the meantime you and your spouse can begin doing things today to get you closer to your trip. You can set aside time together to discuss your plans. Maybe it's a morning walk before breakfast or a night out at your favorite restaurant. Maybe it only happens once a month, but on that walk or during that dinner you remember your friendship. You enjoy each other's company. You might still be in your old neighborhood, but together you are creating an experience. Maybe you order that second bottle of wine. Maybe it starts to rain and you run home together laughing. Together you end up creating memories from these small outings that will be shared for the rest of your lives. Experiences like this can be built into your every day; little things as well as big can and should be planned for if you want to enter into the realm of the RichLife. You can start living out your bucket list *today*.

The Laughing Corner

In the small town of Solon Springs, Wisconsin, a group of people meet regularly on a street corner. They have been featured in newspapers and live newscasts nationwide. They call themselves *the laughing group* and they meet every Sunday at an appointed time, on the corner of a street, with one purpose in mind—to laugh. The group has grown to about thirty people strong, with an average of twelve people meeting every week. Over the years they have spent laughing together on that corner, they have shared a fair amount of intimate stories and done a bit of crying, too. But always the spirit of the group and the intention to laugh takes over. Because of this planned intention, everyone always leaves feeling better. It is a testament to the importance of organizing an event, and a good example of how valuable experiences can be created without any monetary investment at all. The laughing group still meets every Sunday, and though some of them are well into their eighties now, they are all still laughing.

Backyard Staycations

Before he became a published author, Paul couldn't afford to take his family on a summer vacation. So he bought a tent and set aside a week each summer to go camping. At first these camping trips were right in their back yard, because it made more sense to spend the gas money on supplies. They built a fire pit and roasted marshmallows; they played flashlight tag and ghost in the grave-yard; they stayed up late talking in their tent and created great family memories together. When Paul finally sold the movie rights to his third book, he took the family on a two-week trip to the Grand Canyon. They stayed in hotels and enjoyed the luxury of swimming pools and continental breakfasts, but most of all they enjoyed each other's company. This was possible and enjoyable because of all the experiences they had shared together *before* he "struck it big."

Little Boxes on the Counter

Irene worried about what to do with her granddaughter, Lucy. Irene wanted to come up with something really terrific because Lucy's other grandma had taken her to Florida where she had a time share in a condo. Irene's economic situation was a lot differ-ent, so when Lucy got back from the trip, Irene questioned the girl, looking for clues as to how she could "one-up" the experience.

"Well? What was it like? What did you do? Was it fun?" she asked.

"Oh, yes," replied the granddaughter. "Every morning for breakfast, we had these little boxes of cereal. They were all differ-ent kinds and Grandma would line them up on the counter and we got to pick whichever one we wanted!"

The magic of a great experience is oftentimes created through the little things. Like Lucy's miniature boxes of cereal, it doesn't always require large amounts of money. Oftentimes the spontaneous outings are the ones we remember best. Whether laughing on a corner or camping in the back yard, setting aside *the time* to spend is how these memories are created. You can begin doing that now, today, regardless of how much you've accumulated in the bank. You wouldn't necessarily think that a little box of cereal could become a lifelong memory, but the truth is it can—if you schedule it in.

DARING TO BE BIG

I have to add here that it is very easy to not do these things. Many people just let the days, weeks, and years slip on by. We all get busy; we get caught up in other plans. As John Lennon once wrote, "Life is what happens while we're busy making other plans." If all your trips and experiences remain as plans to be done in the future, life *will* just *happen,* and you're right back to playing the *when I, then I* game. The years will march by and valuable opportunities will be lost. Those things that you always meant to get around to doing will in the end go undone, and the people with whom you could have done them will grow distant. You can do something about that. You can begin creating your own life field trips that will put rich memories into your relationship bank account.

With regard to creating unique experiences on purpose, the key is to start now by doing small things while planning together for the big.

You will be drawn closer together, and in the process create the wealth of shared experience, of *memories.* These memories will greatly add to the value of your relationship accounts, making those investments even stronger.

Experiences also strengthen the relationship you have with yourself. This ties back to the idea of having a life purpose. Are you having the experience of life that you want to have? Are you getting the most out of your time here on earth? Do you have a dream?

THE DREAMERS AND THE DOERS

Sussil Liyanage was born to a middle class rural family in Yak-wewa Medawachchiya, a tiny village in Sri Lanka. Coming from a developing nation and with no knowledge of English, it was an amazing feat that he ended up selling insurance in New York City as partner for New York Life. Sussil was living in one of the richest cities in the world and earning a salary of $180,000 a year, when he realized that he was not getting the experience he wanted out of life. In his own words, Sussil explains:

> I was alone in New York. I had money but no family. I had a job but no life purpose. I had a good salary, but I wanted to have everything: family, good health, my values. That's why I came back. I realized I had to reset everything in order to have the experience of a balanced life.

Sussil found the balance he sought when he decided that he had a calling to help his country. It wasn't that the people of Sri Lanka needed new information; it was that they needed a new experience of what their life could be about. Sussil explains:

> The country had been at war for the last 30 years, and the people of Sri Lanka forgot how to dream. They forgot a lot of things because of the bombings, and they lost their purpose in life. Many people also lost their

good health. I saw that I had an opportunity to practice what I believe. To not just inform, but to transform. To be the message: You can do more things, you can do better things.

Sussil embraced the opportunity to experience a larger version of his life. He saw that he could do a lot of practical good by learning how to do things better, and then sharing that experience with the people of Sri Lanka.

Sussil left New York City and went back to his country. He engaged in behavior changing activities to become a better financial advisor, embarking on a mission to not just advise, but to experience and teach. Through his own example of transformation, achieving a balance of relationships, health, wealth, and life purpose, he became the example of the RichLife he now teaches others how to build.

I wanted to learn better things, how to become a better financial advisor, and how to deliver complete advice. Now I do all the programs for RichLife international. I ask people, "What is your mission? What is your story? What is your goal for the next ten years? Where are you going to be in mind, body, heart and spirit?" I also ask people, "How many miles can you run in one hour?" And I ask them to tell me, "What is the picture in your mind?" If that person doesn't have a picture, then that person cannot go there.

Sussil also works with the youth of Sri Lanka, teaching them the building blocks of true wealth in a program called Leaders for Life. He shows them not just how to manage their finances, but how to build a solid foundation on which to grow and nurture their own definition of a RichLife.

In order for transformation to happen, people have to be involved. Anyone can get the information, but for transformation, you have to be doing things. In our programs, we do many behavior-changing activities in order to provide this opportunity to transform.

Sussil could have stayed in New York, enjoying his very comfortable life, but he would have missed out on the experience of his life that he is enjoying today.

Now I have good health, good family, and I play with my kids. I am making good money helping people and I have that feeling. The feeling of a RichLife.

But Sussil is stopping there? No, he's got bigger plans:

We have 22 million people in this country. My goal is to directly help 1 million of my people to achieve their definition of a RichLife in the next 10 years.

Yes, the world needs dreamers, but until you add action to the dream, it is just a great idea. The good news is that a doer is simply a dreamer who takes action. It's a maturation process that sets some on the course to do great things and create tremendous value in the lives of others and in the world. *This is the bigger context of creating meaningful experiences. It's the macro-view of your own life.* What do you want your experience here to mean? Will those experiences remain in your mind, as dreams, or will you flip the switch and become a doer?

There is nothing more tragic than a dreamer who does nothing and nothing more powerful than a dreamer who takes action.

THE RICHLIFE EXPERIENCE

As a RichLife advisor, it has always been important to not just to talk about creating experiences, but to also provide opportunities for them. I have had many people in my life provide those opportunities for me. My father was one of the first, and he taught me the value of investing in relationships. Over the years, the thousands of clients I have spoken with who shared their stories taught me the value of creating experiences. From them, I learned that investments in doing things form life's greatest asset—*lasting memories*. One way that I can give back, contributing to the strength of relationships and experiences in the lives of others, is by not only teaching the RichLife philosophy, but also by providing opportunities for other people to kick-start their own version of a RichLife.

To that end, I have created the "RichLife Experience" as one way I can share with like-minded clients and friends invested in the RichLife philosophy. We take a group of ten to twelve people on a "field trip" designed to give everyone in attendance a unique and fulfilling experience. Some examples are a Costa Rican canopy tour and rafting trip, sky diving, or building clean water supply in the Dominican Republic. These trips might also include seminars, mission work, coaching, and intensive training from some of the top minds in the world. I consider these trips a success when memories are created and new relationships forged that last a lifetime.

I also encourage you to seek out opportunities that can serve others, expanding any limiting ideas you might have while tackling some of the things on your bucket list. When you do, I hope you will tell me about the experiences you create. I would love to hear about them.

PORTFOLIO BUILDER

In my interviews with thousands of people over the years, I have learned firsthand that a life lived without unique experiences is mediocre, lacking in joy and vibrancy, and often filled with regret. Looking back, there is no amount of money that can buy memories and experiences after the fact. Look around at your own life. What joyous occasions are you missing out on simply because you're not factoring unique experiences into the mix? No canvas equals no painting. It seldom happens by accident. The difference between the dreamers and the doers is the action. Creating unique experiences requires an intentional plan.

Set up the canvas, grab the paints, get ready for some fun. Unique experiences are painted against the blank canvas that *you* provide and set up. I look forward to hearing about what you create.

 THE TAKE-AWAYS

- Though not every field trip is a life-changing event, trips have the potential to create lifelong memories.

- Unique experiences, shared or alone, become our memories, and these are the most valuable assets you can own.

- To create your own unique experiences and memories, begin now by doing small things and plan together for the big.

- Transformation is about more than just getting information. It's about using that information to fully experience life.

- The world needs dreamers, but until you add action to the dream, it is just a good idea. By adding action to your dreams you will enjoy a richer version of life.

ACTION STEPS

- Create your own bucket list. Write down ten unique experiences or things that you would like to do before your time on earth is over. When you make your bucket list, do so without regard to how or when. Dream big. The sky is the limit.

- List one small unique experience you can easily create this week. Set aside the time to do it, and take one concrete step toward its implementation. For example: invite a friend to meet you for a run, buy a beginner's piano book and start learning a song, or plan a surprise night out for your spouse, arranging the babysitter and making the dinner reservations.

- Choose one of the big experiences listed on your bucket list and pick one concrete thing you can do this week toward the planning of this event. For example: pick up the application for a passport at your local post office, check out some library books on travelling in Italy, or sign up for skiing lessons.

- Challenge: Take action and intentionally turn one of your great ideas into the beginnings of an experience. Make it easy for yourself by choosing an action that you can do. By taking a small action, you will begin experiencing your idea. For example, if you have the dream of building an indoor gym facility for autistic kids, get a notebook, put a label on it, and start brainstorming.

- **Bonus Gift**: Find all of the above exercises by downloading your free copy of the Action Guide for *The RichLife: Ten Investments for True Wealth* at www.RichLifeActionGuide.com.

MASTER YOUR MONEY MAP

"In macroeconomics, success or failure is not due to the performance of the investment. It is always due to the efficiency of the investor."

—ANDREW ROSENBAUM, author of
The Wealth Swing Coach

YOU ARE HERE!

We are now at the halfway point of the book and the time has come to talk about some basic financial principles. We are going to get started by taking a look at where you are with regard to your finances. When using a GPS system in your car to map out a road trip, you must have two pieces of information. First, *you must know your destination*—or where you are going. Second, and equally as important, *you must know where you are now*. This is your starting point. Without knowing those two pieces of information—your present position and your destination—there's no way you can map a course.

Your RichLife is where you are going. But before we can get you there, we must figure out where you are right now with regard to money. A lot of people don't want to take a close look at their finances. They either don't have the time, think it will be too depressing, or are afraid of the changes that may be required of them. The truth is, *not* looking at your finances causes much more of an energy drain than the time it takes to get clear about your numbers. And you won't be able to reach your end destination with any certainty without a clear starting point.

Let's look at it another way. If you go into a shopping mall and you want to go to McDonald's, the first thing you do is locate the mall directory stationed at the main entrance. On the directory you'll find a little red star that says, "You arc here!" Only then can you figure out which direction to go to get to McDonald's. Without that little red star, any movement you made would be inefficient. Any direction you chose would be a random shot in the dark. You might walk for hours, wasting all your energy going in the exact opposite direction. You might stumble on the store eventually, but you'd have no idea how you did it. You wouldn't be able to get there again with any certainty, and you wouldn't be able to help anybody else get there. When this metaphor is applied to your life and finances, we could be talking about years of poor money management and hundreds of thousands of dollars spent inefficiently.

Taking a good look at where you are now is the first step in mapping out the journey for a successful financial future. Most people are just hoping things will work out. They figure if they work hard and keep at it, the money will take care of itself. In my career as a financial advisor, I have seen scores of business owners and individuals who appear successful and on top of their game, but do not know exactly what is coming in and what is going out on any given month. If you are nodding your head, you are not alone. The overwhelming majority of people do not know where they stand with their finances.

ON SIGHT

When Shawn and his wife Krista started their photography business, they were excited to have identified a specific niche—on location photography for students involved in sports. They named their company On Sight, invested in a professional, high-resolution printer, and set up a slick online ordering system for the parents. It was the beginning of hockey season in the upper Midwest, and they were booked solid, shooting games every weekend and downloading the photographs to their website. Shawn focused on the photography, taking the pictures, fine-tuning and cropping the images, and constantly updating the website. Krista secured future bookings and managed the printing and shipment of the orders.

The business took off right away. Shawn's pictures were good and their price point was in line with what parents were willing to pay. The hours Shawn spent in the ice arenas began to pay off. By the end of their first month, On Sight had an impressive amount of capital flowing into their bank account. One afternoon, the president of the bank himself came out to meet Shawn in the lobby. They shook hands and he congratulated Shawn on the success of the business. By the end of their first year, Shawn and Krista had deposited more than $300,000 in funds, and On Sight was deemed a huge success.

As the season for winter sports started up again the following year, Shawn booked himself and his wife on a flight to Colorado where they would shoot several high-profile skiing events. The gig would look impressive on their website and was a big, three-day weekend event. But when Shawn charged the plane tickets to his business credit card, the transaction was unexpectedly declined.

"I had no idea how it happened. We were making so much money, it didn't seem possible that we could have spent more than what was coming in. But we were so focused on the success of the company, we said 'yes' to everything, every booking, every engagement, and every opportunity. We never stopped to look at what it would cost and to ask if there was enough in our budget. We didn't even *have* a budget!"

MICRO VERSES MACRO

In the case of Shawn and Krista, a budget wasn't what they needed. A lot of people make the mistake of thinking that creating a budget is the first step when really it is only a tool. A budget can only help you if you know where you are and where you want to go. In other words, *you must have the whole picture*. What happened with On Sight is a common business mistake that I have seen many times. Decisions about money are made in the moment, *based on what is easiest or cheapest now* as opposed to what will create a more favorable future. This short-sighted view of money is called *microeconomics*. Money is spent or saved without considering future repercussions or how it affects the picture as a whole.

Going back to our shopping analogy, micro-decisions would be buying the cheap, disposable versions of things instead of investing in lasting, more permanent options. It will result in the need to buy that item again, which requires more of your time and more of your assets. While sometimes it does make sense to save a few bucks today and buy the cheaper item, *the micro view of money often leads to an erosion of financial stability over the long term*. This is because every financial decision *does* affect the picture of the whole. Seemingly little mistakes over time add up to big errors. They can go undetected and eat away at your future unless you take the time now to focus on your numbers.

Without identifying both your starting point and your destination, your money decisions won't be grounded. You will be adrift, directionless, and at the mercy of the economy. You will be reacting instead of directing your life. We can think of the micro/macro model as the difference between staying focused on the raft versus focused on the shore. With the micro view of money, all that matters is the raft, or where you are today. You only take care of the raft, and so your direction is left to the mercy of the river. The river can be likened to the economy. When it is rough, you will be having a miserable ride. When things are going well, the sailing will be smooth. Either way, it's vital to the health of your financial future to know where, exactly, you are headed.

With the macro view of money, your focus is on the end goal of reaching shore. You need to take care of your raft and stay current on repairs, yes. But decisions about whether or not to invest in the raft will be calculated based on how much further you have to go. It wouldn't make sense to buy a sail, for example, if you are so close to land that all you have to do is hop out and drag the raft onto the sand.

Going back to the business started by Shawn and Krista, had they started with the bigger picture in mind, they would have managed their income differently. The trouble here was that they never took the time to identify what that bigger picture was. The general idea of success and knowing how much money is coming into the bank is not the same thing as a money map. In the end, Shawn and Krista did file for bankruptcy. Together they owed a mind-boggling amount of money in business credit card debt and loans. They were paying the bills from last month with what they were earning at the current booking and had no idea where they stood financially at any given point. With their microeconomic view—no plan and no budget—they took on too much too soon, and found themselves in way over their heads.

KNOW YOUR NUMBERS

Beginning with the end in mind and knowing what is coming in and what is going out is more than just good advice—*it's essential to reaching your destination.* Most people have a little money tucked away in savings; others may have done a little investing in mutual funds or real estate. Some people live on a fixed income or receive regular paychecks, while others work on a per project basis, receiving sales commissions. But none of the numbers are concrete. The income and expenses for each month are unknown. For the most part, people are just *hoping* that everything works out all right. This strategy—if you can call it that—is as follows: "I've done a little here and a little there. And I work hard. *I hope* when I get to the time of financial need at some point in the future, it will all just work out."

When it comes to prosperity, hoping doesn't cut it. It sets up the conditions of wanting something that isn't there, and these conditions are then perpetuated through simple avoidance or ignorance. Hoping puts someone else in charge. Knowing puts you in the driver's seat. Even if you have no gift for numbers, there is no reason why you can't take charge of your finances today. In order to create the conditions favorable to reaching your desired destination, you must begin with where you are now, and that means doing the work of learning how much money is coming in, how much is going out, the total of your assets, and the total of your liabilities. Just like using a GPS system or entering a shopping mall, without a starting point any movement made toward your destination will be inefficient and at best a gamble. Why take such an unnecessary risk when you don't have to? When it comes to financial success, you need to bite the bullet now and do the work to create your Money Map. This map will tell you where you are financially, and from there you can drive your life forward to wherever it is you want to go.

I am happy to say that Shawn and Krista have their act together now. They recovered, learned their lesson from life school, and took the time to restructure and map out their finances instead of focusing solely on the income. It doesn't matter if you're earning one hundred dollars or one million if that same amount is being spent simultaneously. Shawn and Krista started over, and this time they have the big picture, *with both a beginning and an end point in mind.*

CREATING YOUR MONEY MAP

The first step to creating your Money Map is to work on two important financial statements—your balance sheet and your income statement. The balance sheet will give you a snapshot in time, so to speak, showing you where you stand with regard to assets and liabilities. Your income statement shows you the cash flow, or what is coming in and going out in any given month. These two statements together give you an accurate reading of where you stand financially. For most people, this work is not fun and the reality is that most personality types will never even do this exercise. The good news, however, is that the work doesn't have to be done by *you*.

Be honest with yourself here. I'm a financial planner and even though I work with numbers for a living, I pay someone a monthly fee to keep my receipts and expenses current with my income. If the thought of working on financial statements makes your skin crawl, that's okay! There are people out there who do this kind of work. There are people for whom bookkeeping is their life purpose. Many of my clients pay a bookkeeper as little as $100 a month to deliver current financial statements. For individuals who run their own business and keep track of daily receipts and expenditures, having this kind of service done for you can be a lifesaver. Others might select a one-time fee and have someone show them how or install a service such as QuickBooks™. Or they might learn how to do it themselves by spending some time online with tools such as Mint˚, Microsoft Money, or YNAB™ (You Need a Budget). For others, the situation might best be served by a good old-fashioned ledger book and pencil.

It doesn't matter how you do it. It only matters that it gets done. In order to achieve financial success, *you need to know your numbers.* Delegate the task if it is something that is not your strength. Knowing your numbers will put you ahead of over 90 percent of your peers and competitors and will help you map out the path to your definition of a fulfilling financial future based on certainty, not luck.

CASH FLOW IS KING

Your **income statement** will have two sides, one side with what comes in, or income, and the other side with what goes out, or expenses. To get a clear idea of what is going out, look at your credit card statements as well as your paper receipts. Include necessary expenses such as fuel for both your car and yourself, and any monthly bills for things such as your phone and Internet, car and health insurance. Also include a category for repairs and maintenance. Factor in an amount that will cover regular oil changes and other maintenance procedures including new tires. Create yet another miscellaneous category to include unexpected expenses such as birthday presents and gifts

Keeping track of your income will be different for everybody in that some of us have steady salaries and predictable paychecks, while others don't. If you are self-employed, work on a commission basis, or have seasonal employment, your income will need to be based on an average. To find that number will require a little bit of digging, but it will be worth it. Calculate your average monthly income by looking at last year's taxes, or by factoring in all income streams, even those whose yields are unpredictable, and dividing by twelve to find an average. Having a number like that can help you put aside the correct amount of money during times of heavy cash flow to cover during the leaner months.

The next financial statement, a **balance sheet**, will calculate your net worth. Your net worth will change over longer periods of time, as the value of what you own increases or decreases depending on the market, and more of your loans are paid off, decreasing your liability. The balance sheet will help give you an accurate picture of where you stand with regard to *what you own and what you owe* using two categories, *assets* and *liabilities*. Assets are those physical items you own which have a calculated worth in dollars. They include vehicles, real estate, and tools or equipment. Liabilities would include all financial obligations which must be met every month such as the mortgage and loan payments. If your business is *renting* a space, then it is not liable for the rent should the business decide to fold or change locations. The monthly rent would be listed as an "expense" and calculated as a bill. If the business *owns* its place of operation, then this building would be an asset, increasing its overall net worth. If the business has a *loan* for the building it owns, then the property would be listed as both an asset and a liability, the building being the asset and the mortgage or loan being the liability. Over time, the balance would shift as you make payments. You will own more of the property as you pay off the principal of the loan, decreasing your liability while increasing your assets.

Once you have tallied the numbers, take a look at the totals. How much is coming in each month? How much is going out? If you need an extra $100 a month to put aside for a college fund, maybe all you need to do is cut out the five trips to Starbucks every week and bring a thermos of coffee from home. Maybe some of your assets have turned into liabilities you can't really afford. Or maybe you are in better shape than you thought you would be. The bottom line is—*now you know.*

BORROWING A LIFESTYLE

When Paul's wife passed away at the age of thirty-six, he went into a tailspin of grief. Not only had he lost his life partner and friend, but they'd had a daughter together. Rebecca was only ten, and now she was left without a mother. That thought overwhelmed Paul. He in no way felt prepared to fill the shoes his wife left empty.

At the beginning there were friends and many offers of help. Paul got his daughter through it, taking it day by day. He did whatever it took to get them from point A to point B with as little suffering as possible. If it was raining, he and Rebecca took a cab. If it was a school night and they hadn't eaten dinner, they would go out some place nice. If she needed a dress to wear for a school concert, he ordered one online and had it delivered overnight. Whatever the cost, it didn't matter. Paul was just going through the grieving process, and as the single parent to a young girl, he needed to do it with as much grace and dignity as possible.

A year went by, and then another. Paul was back in the full swing of his life, working a steady and regular job as a property surveyor. Rebecca was now almost a teenager and had taken up an interest in horses. The spending habits he had developed during the past two years didn't change. He bought his daughter a horse they couldn't afford and found a place to board it. She began taking regular riding lessons at $60 an hour, three times a week. Soon after that she wanted to enter her horse in shows, and Paul couldn't say no.

When things started to get tight, Paul financed a home equity line of credit. That gave him and his daughter some breathing room for another year. Meanwhile he continued to spend money so they could have the best of everything. Every two years he bought a newer car; they got another horse so that he could go on rides with her. Eventually they even bought a trailer so she could travel to out-of-state shows.

When things got tight again, he sold a piece of real estate. This went on for ten years until Rebecca graduated from high school and went on to college. With his daughter out of the house, things got very quiet. The retirement years loomed up ahead on the horizon. Paul took a look around at his financial affairs and realized he was in no way prepared. When the property taxes came due, he struggled to make the payment.

"It's this economy!" he complained. "It's a bad market!"

Yet when he finally got all of his finances together and took a look at where he stood, Paul learned that he had been outspending his income for years

Live Below Your Means

It is very easy to charge things on a credit card. It is also easy to fall into the trap of trying to impress people with a lifestyle you can't afford. It is human nature to want to give the best to your children, your friends, even to yourself. But the only way to achieve the balance of health and the full wealth of all the assets—human, physical and financial—is by investing in the big picture. Knowing where you are going will keep you from the temptation of borrowing a lifestyle that doesn't take you where you want to go. Even if it is possible to do everything you want to do in the moment and still make it work, as Paul did, in the end you will have nothing left to show for it. You will not get to your final destination.

I have a client who lives on the outskirts of town and works on old rural homes, updating their plumbing. Morgan is a straightforward, blue-collar kind of guy, but with tremendous saving habits. His net worth is two to three times greater than some of my highest earning clients, yet he doesn't dress in designer suits. He also isn't stressed by his lifestyle. One of the more interesting things I've noticed over the years is that the most financially secure people are those who don't feel the need to use their money as leverage. In other words, their appearance doesn't unnecessarily advertise their wealth. Their success allows them to live in a way that suits them, without having to impress others, and they are among the happiest, most easygoing people I know

One thing I ask my clients to do is to envision their lives as they would like to see them ten years from now. Now we did this in a previous chapter with regard to designing your RichLife, but doing so with regard to your finances will help you to develop a *macroeconomic* mindset. Ten years is long enough to accomplish some pretty big things, yet small enough to picture clearly. The time will also go by faster than you'd ever expect it. If you have a clear picture of where you want to be, it becomes easier to say "no" to the things you can't afford now like a new car or a bigger house. You can look at that new car and say, "I'd rather not have a car payment." You can look at that bigger house and say, "I'd rather have the weekend off, kneeling in the dirt and planting tulips with my granddaughter."

Once you have done the work and understand your numbers, it is essential that you live within those means. One of the great secrets to building wealth *is to live below your means*. Even though you *can* go out to dinner, you don't. Even though you *can* afford a higher car payment, you invest that money differently. You put it to work for you so that ten years from now, you achieve the picture of your RichLife. Whether you are earning $150,000 a year or $20,000, you *can* become wealthy if you have more coming in than going out.

We live in a time of plenty—plenty of food, plenty of choices, plenty of credit cards. On any given day we are surrounded by more calories than we need, yet we don't consume them all. We choose instead a diet that will support a healthy body and build a healthy immune system. We say yes to some things and no to others. The doctors tell us to stop eating just before we become too full. As your financial planner, I am telling you the same thing with regard to your money. Choose to stop spending before you have spent everything. Choose to keep things comfortable for yourself by living below your means. This will support a healthy financial future

THE TRUTH ABOUT MONEY

To conclude our chapter about money, I would like to take a close look at what money really is. I've seen a lot of people who are pretty confused about money. They risk everything to get more of it because they believe that it has the power to make them happy. Like Sussil Liyanage from the previous chapter, maybe you have also discovered for yourself that money alone does not give you a complete life.

I admit that money is a powerful word. The promise of it has the ability to make people do and say crazy things. But the bottom line here is that building a truly rich and fulfilled life requires that we keep money in its proper place. We must remember what it really is.

On my radio show and during seminars, I talk a lot about *the truth of dead presidents on paper.* Because really, when it comes right down to it, that's all money is. Money in and of itself has no intrinsic value. It is merely a tool with which to *measure* value. If you have something of value and I want to purchase that item from you, in our society I give you money for it. In America that would be dollars. In Sri Lanka, it would rupees. In many other parts of the world, it would be euros. In centuries past I might have given you gold doubloons, a pretty shell, a belt of beaded wampum, or even salt. Money is a medium of exchange. To think of money in this way may require a paradigm shift from what you have heard all your life. If you are looking at your income statement and thinking, *I need more money!* that thought likely makes you tense and anxious, so keep in mind where you want to go and what you want to achieve. Remember that money is only a tool and should never take priority over the people it was meant to serve.

Instead of thinking about acquiring money, focus on utilizing your assets and resources to move you toward your goals and objectives. Build on that as your foundation. Money can then have a greater impact on the things in life that are truly fulfilling. It can then be of service to you, instead of you being the one serving it. By viewing money this way, your thoughts about it will undergo a shift. Instead of focusing on accumulating money, you are adding value to your life. My experience is that only the latter can produce long-term financial success and a fulfilled and balanced life.

THE TRUTH ABOUT INVESTMENTS

Another question I get asked a lot concerns what to do with money. Individuals come to me and ask the vague question of, "What is the best investment?" Or they ask me specific questions such as, "Should I invest in stocks? In bonds, gold, real estate, businesses, etc.?"

My answer: In order to know, I'll have to ask you a lot more questions. I need more information."

The value of an investment has to do with the financial goals and objectives of the investor. In other words, there is no best investment.

While most people focus on trying to find the best investment, true success comes when you realize that all investments are *neutral*. It is neither a winner nor a loser for any one person. In fact, two different people can be set up in the exact same investment—one might come out with huge gains and the other end up broke. In other words, each investor begins from a different place, has a different destination in mind, and a different financial IQ. What must be clear from the outset are the particular situations and the long-term objectives of the investor. In other words, each investor *begins from a different place*, and each one has *a different destination* in mind. In order to choose "the best investment," you must be clear about those two things first.

Let's take a look at a case in point. Do you remember my client David from our chapter about clarity? When I asked him *why* he wanted to invest in real estate, his answer was, "Because there are some great deals out there now." He'd been reading about how to pick up foreclosed houses at deep discounts. While this was true, I pressed him further.

"*Why* do you want to invest in real estate?" I continued to present the same question, and he gave me vague answers until he realized he wasn't really getting to the heart of things. His answer wasn't really solid. He thought about it for a minute, and then finally he replied, "I want to invest in real estate because five years from now, I don't want to be working at my job anymore."

Well, now we were getting somewhere. But I wasn't finished. My next question was, "*Why* do you want to retire in five years?" This might sound like an unnecessary question, but everyone has a different idea about what retirement really is. Everyone has an objective in mind, even if they themselves haven't said it out loud. We kept drilling down with more specific questions until it was finally revealed that he needed $3,000 a month to supplement his income so he could stay home and help raise his granddaughter. He had identified caring for and spending time with his granddaughter, at this point in his life, as his new definition of a RichLife.

Now we could begin to map a course for him to reach his goals and objectives. Had we begun investing in real estate without this valuable interchange, things could have gotten way off course. The type of real estate David had been considering would have been totally wrong for his particular situation, and if he had used it he might never have reached his financial objective in the time frame he envisioned. This happens all the time—people hear something on the news or read about it in the newspaper and they're ready to base their investment program on something that "sounds good."

Let's go back to the analogy of using a GPS to map your road trip. Choosing an investment program before you are clear on your objectives is like starting out in Atlanta, Georgia and you want to go to San Diego, California, but instead of heading west you go north toward Buffalo, New York, because you heard on the news it was a great place to visit right now! It makes no sense, yet a lot of people fall for it. With regard to investments, your definition of a RichLife is located at the end of your biggest why.

The best way to map your investment strategy is to ask yourself "why" until you can't ask it any more. This will get you to the heart of your motivation. Once that is identified, you can plan a strategy designed to move you *toward* your desired destination.

IS IT WORTH THE COST?

In the same way that money is neutral and investments are neutral, so too are those things we choose to buy. You might look at your neighbor's boat sitting up on blocks in the backyard and think to yourself, "Wow, what a waste of money." But what if living on a houseboat is their idea of a dream retirement? You can look at any purchases you make with the same paradigm shift we described earlier. Purchasing grown-up toys like boats and snowmobiles is neither good nor bad. They will simply either serve you or not. The purchase will either help move you *toward* your goals or move you *away* from those goals. Looking at purchasing decisions in this way will help make your decisions with clarity instead of judgment.

I would like to leave you with some good advice I learned from my friend and mentor, Steven D'Annunzio. A good rule of thumb to apply to any purchasing decision, be it large or small, is to ask: Is the price worth the cost? In other words, is the price of what I am doing today worth the cost in the future? If you keep the big picture in mind, the answer to that question should help you stay the course toward destination RichLife.

 ## PORTFOLIO BUILDER

We covered some valuable ground in this chapter with regard to finances. I hope you understand the importance of knowing your numbers. Before you can begin moving toward your RichLife, you must first identify where it is you are now with regard to your finances. Like the "You Are Here" star on maps, knowing your starting point can help you to more efficiently reach your destination. Once you have identified your destination, you can then more efficiently manage the assets that you do have, allowing the money to serve you so that you can embark in a straight line to wherever it is you want to go.

THE TAKE-AWAYS

- Create your Money Map by having an income statement and balance sheet prepared, either by yourself or by a professional.

- A shortsighted view of money is called *microeconomics*, where money is used without considering how it affects the picture of the whole. This view of money always leads to an erosion of finances over the long term.

- To achieve full wealth of all the assets—human, physical, and financial—invest in the big picture, or *macroeconomics*.

- One of the great secrets to building wealth is to live below your means.

- Money by itself is neutral, as are investments and purchases. Ask yourself if the *price* is worth what it will *cost you down the road* with regard to your future goals and objectives.

 ## ACTION STEPS

- Chart your course: Ask yourself where you would like to be ten years from now with regard to your finances. Ask yourself "why" until you get to the bottom, and then write down your answer. Form a concise, one-sentence answer to the question: What is my destination?

- Create your Money Map: Get together all the financial documents you need to get a clear picture of your finances *now*. Create both an income statement and a balance sheet as described earlier in this chapter. You can access a free money map template at BeauHenderson.com or hire someone in your area to help you.

- Design your lifestyle: The first two action exercises will give you both your starting point and your destination. You are now ready to make the trip. Design a budget that you and your family can stick to. Make sure that it follows the principles of macroeconomics by keeping the bigger picture in mind. Get everybody in the household on board so tempting purchases are put into perspective. If time is set aside for relationships and fun experiences, living below your means will not seem like a hardship at all.

- **Bonus Gift**: Download your free copy of the Action Guide for *The RichLife: Ten Investments for True Wealth* at www.RichLifeActionGuide.com.

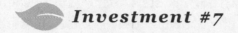 *Investment #7*

CHOOSE RISK TRANSFER

"A man who fears suffering is already
suffering from what he fears."

—Michel Montaigne,
French Renaissance writer

STEWARDSHIP OF MONEY

The funny thing about accumulating money is that the more of
it you have, the more you feel yourself to be at risk. This is true of
all our financial assets and most of the physical ones as well, including our homes, our cars, and our lifestyle. The more you have, the
more you stand to lose. And the more vulnerable you are to thieves.

Thieves can come in many forms. They can arrive as an illness,
a disability, or lack of knowledge regarding new tax laws. They can
come in the form of premature death, inflation, or gradual erosion.
Thieves can also show up in the form of other people, but for most
of us, when it comes to the majority of our assets, stereotypical bur-
glars are the least of our worries.

Enjoying your RichLife will not be possible if every penny of it remains at risk. So what can you do? What can be done to mitigate this fear and restore peace of mind?

In Investment #1, we took a good look at the concept of wise stewardship. We learned that stewardship and responsibility are closely related, and that the word *stewardship* comes from the root word *keeper.* We are now going to take a look at how to practice wise stewardship with regard to our financial assets. We are going to talk about investing, specifically financial planning, and the transferring of risk.

But we have to bust many of the myths we have come to believe with regard to sound financial investing. We are going to clear up some of these fallacies and find a better way that will allow you to keep more of what you have while giving you a greater peace of mind. Now, I invite you to imagine the following scene with me:

LAS VEGAS SCENARIO

You and your family are spending your long-planned-for vacation in Las Vegas, and here you are, walking down the infamous Strip. You enter a popular casino with money jingling in your pocket, ready to spend a few hours playing a few games.

A gentleman greets you at the front door, welcomes you in and tells you that he wants to *help* you. "I've been involved with casinos for years," he explains, "and I know all the ins and outs. I know the intricacies of all the games —blackjack, five card draw, slots, keno, roulette, stud poker—you name it, I can make it profitable for you."

You are impressed with his pitch, and he seems very pleasant and poised, so you don't walk away. You tell him instead that you were headed for the nickel slots, and that later you might try your hand at keno though you've never played that before. He smiles and nods and says "Okay, great. That all sounds good. How much money would you like me to play?" It's at that point you realize he wants to *take* your money and play the games *for* you! You look around at the faces of your family. But then the gentleman adds, "Just tell me your *risk tolerance*. I'll use that to make any decisions about what games I play, how much I put in, and for how long." Then he adds, "I want you to be able to enjoy yourself!"

Well, you've never heard of such a thing and would like to see a little proof. Does he have any testimonies? How about a record of past history with regard to rendering this *service* to people?

"Oh yes," he replies, and promptly pulls out a spread sheet and shows you his average *rate of return* over a period of ten to twenty years. Well, he's experienced. And it doesn't look too bad when you look at it stretched over that amount of time. In fact, it seems he is able to produce more gains than losses, and this, after all, is only your second visit to Las Vegas. You aren't exactly a card shark. But still, you have other questions:

Can he promise you that he will win you money?

No. There is always the chance that he might lose.

Can you at least *watch* this representative as he distributes your money around the casino?

The answer is no.

Do you get to tell him where you would like your money to be played?

Not exactly.

Do you have any input *at all* into how this gambling venture is played out?

You guessed it—no!

"Sounds risky," you say.

And the man agrees with a grin.

"High risk equals high return! You won't get much for your money at those nickel slots. A ten percent rate of return at best. But with me playing at the higher stakes games, the potential return on your total investment go up to forty percent or fifty percent and in some cases, even more. "

But wait, it gets even better. Our suave professional saves the best for last. With a flick of his wrist and a flare of the hand, he bows and promises, "All of the profits that I make for you today will be available to you in cash funds *approximately six months from now.*"

What? Six months from now?

"But can't I have it any sooner?" you ask. "I was planning on using my wins today to pay for part of this vacation."

"Sure, you can have it sooner," he replies, "no problem. But I'll have to charge you a hefty penalty for that."

A hefty penalty?

"But it was my money to begin with! I gave it to you!"

"That's right. So I'm happy to do it for you, if that's what you need. The penalty will just come right off the top of your winnings."

Looking around at the casino, you notice what everybody else is doing. They are all handing over their money at the door. In fact, you don't see anybody entering the casino without first having this same kind of exchange. Well, if that's what everybody else is doing, what are you waiting for? Today could be your lucky day! You reach into your wallet and before the cocktail waitress can offer you a drink, you've already signed up and handed over the funds.

INVESTING OR GAMBLING?

Most of you are reading this scenario and wondering what planet I just dropped in from. Who in their right mind would ever hand over their money to a complete stranger and let him do with it as he wills? And then keep the profits for a few months to use as he wishes? With no promise or guarantee of a return?

Most people visiting Las Vegas are looking for a good time. They have hopes of winning, but they also expect to lose something for it as well. Believe it or not, this pretty closely describes the retirement funds, IRAs, or 401(k)s of most Americans. Most people approach investing for retirement with a similar mindset, expecting some losses and handing over all their funds at the door. Allow me to walk you through a typical meeting with a financial planner:

After being greeted and shown into the office, he will want to know what assets you have, the amount of your cash flow and how much you'd like to have when you retire. Next, he might have you answer a few questions to learn your *risk tolerance*. This is a clear indicator that he is fully expecting losses along the way, but then again, so are you. You're in this for the long term, right? You understand that high returns require high risk, but hope that in the end, things comes out in your favor. From this information, our financial planner will calculate an amount for you to set aside each month, and for however many years, and throw in a few numbers regarding taxes and interest rates.

You leave the office believing you have done the responsible thing. You are doing what the financial institutions tell you to do so you can achieve the notion of the American Dream. You sink money into stocks or mutual funds (or some other structured type of retirement fund), but typically have no idea what your money is doing. With the focus on accumulating as much money as possible, your financial planner turns around and invests your money in companies you know little, if anything, about. You have no say over what those companies do, and no way to influence their decisions or behaviors. Not only are you denied input as to how your money is used, but you are also not allowed to touch *your money* without incurring a penalty. Your job is to sit back and *watch it being played with.*

RAISING YOUR FINANCIAL IQ

The problem with the scenario I just described above is that investing this way more closely resembles our imagined trip to the casino. You hand over your money to a stranger and trust that they will do the best thing. But your money is your responsibility, and at the end of the day, you are the one who has to live with the results of any risks played out on your behalf. The truth about investments is that their behavior is never more important than yours. What you are doing is more important than what the investment is doing. What you do has a greater chance of increasing a favorable outcome.

So what should you be doing?

I encourage you to ask questions. I have seen it happen countless times where two investors make the exact same investment; one person ends up with a sizeable profit and the other ends up with a loss. What was the difference? You guessed it—the behavior of the investor. One of them got out too soon or bought the stock for the wrong reasons. Other times they stayed in too long or didn't understand the investment.

People ask me, "Is this a good investment?" and I can't give an answer right away because there are more questions to ask. A good financial advisor will ask questions that help you get to the bottom of what you want to do and why.

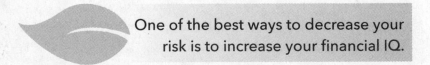

One of the best ways to decrease your risk is to increase your financial IQ.

That means understanding what you are investing in. Most people hand over their money at the door and never bother to learn anything about what they are investing in. Even a mediocre financial planner can help reduce your risk if you learn to ask the right questions. An investment you understand always has less risk than one which you know nothing about.

Do you remember our goose who lays the golden eggs? Investing without first educating yourself can be likened to sending that goose off to board with someone whom you don't even know, and then paying them a set amount every month for food and housing. Meanwhile, you have no recourse should you discover down the road that the goose is poorly sheltered and being starved. If you try to get her back, you will incur so many penalties, she just might end up dead.

Here, I offer a better approach, one that starts by eliminating unnecessary risk to the goose. An approach that increases the chances those golden eggs will keep on giving because the goose has a safe and secure nest. This is not anything new. I am not reinventing the wheel here, but rather employing the wisdom that successful banks and financial institutions have been using for years. They know the secret, and now I'm going to pass it on to you. I am going to teach you what successful banks and corporations have been doing for years to increase their chances of a sizeable profit. It's called transferring risk, and when done right it forms a solid foundation on which to build the investments for your RichLife.

But before we go into all the specifics of how you can effectively transfer the risk to your assets, I'd first like to take a look at a few money myths with regard to investing that we've all come to accept as truth. I'd like to clear up a few of these misconceptions to help clean the lens, so to speak, through which we view our financial world

MYTH # 1: HIGH RISK EQUALS HIGH RETURN

We have all been taught to accept the myth that in order to increase our chances of winning, we must increase our chances of losing. Yet this means one thing—you have a greater chance of losing. This myth was part of my training as a financial planner, and I'm still hearing it today. We've all heard it so often, we don't even think about it anymore. But ask yourself, why would you want to *increase* your chances of losing? The truth is, of course, that you wouldn't.

In essence, the idea of *high risk equals high return* is setting you up to *expect* to lose. As when you enter a casino, you are prepared to simply let some money slip right on down the drain in exchange for your chances at winning big. When you invest in this way, you are essentially providing the capital for other people to take a chance. Your money is serving them, not you, and investing this way is only that—a chance. It is not a guarantee.

The proponents of the *high risk equals high return* theory will also go so far as to suggest that the younger you are, the more risk you can *tolerate.* Translated, this means that you can lose more when you are young, because you have more years to "catch up" before retirement. This is true. You do have more years of earning ahead of you. So you are lulled into thinking that it's okay to be in a losing position, because you can always make it up again. But why should you have to?

To increase your chances of winning, you must decrease your chances of losing.

Most people don't realize that they are more valuable than the money they earn. You are the one with the skills and the know-how; you are the one with the wisdom. So ask yourself: why accept losing as something you have to live with? You worked hard to earn your money. I can assure you that the financial institutions do not operate this way. When they invest, they go to great lengths to minimize any and all risk. They would never operate on the principle that you *can make greater profits by increasing the chances of losing.* Wisdom dictates that it works just the opposite. The most lucrative investments are the least risky. The worst performing investments come with the highest risk.

All financial institutions know this, and by the end of this chapter so will you. Please allow me to introduce a new principle:

This principle is what we build our RichLife investments on. It forms the foundation, the block from which we build up. Risk transfer is not an alternative to investing. It's what comes first.

MYTH #2: THE ACCUMULATION THEORY

Most people go to a financial planner with one goal in mind—to carefully invest earnings for the greatest returns, building toward a secure retirement. Because of this mindset, most financial planners out there are focused mainly on the financial statements—the bottom line of *monetary accumulation*.

The goal here is to stockpile money. Yes, it does feel good to say that you have X amount of money stored up in the bank. But the time has come to ask the question: Is that the best goal? Should accumulation be the highest priority?

People rationalize to themselves that they must accumulate in order to be happy. But building a RichLife is about all of our assets—human, physical, and financial—and money only plays one part of that. Upon closer inspection, most people realize that it's *not having to worry about money* that truly brings them peace and happiness. That is why we have those savings accounts where we set aside money for a rainy day. I am not suggesting that you do away with your savings. I am saying that with regard to investing and planning for the future, the goal should never be *just* about accumulating as much as you can. Here is why.

You could move forward during a series of *good* years and wind up with a sizeable profit. Or you might hit a huge bump in the road and end up with half of what you had to begin with. You know that both scenarios have an equally good chance of happening, and it's all in the timing. You hear about people who planned to retire the very next year and almost overnight they lose half of all they had accumulated. The more money you have invested, the more you stand to lose and the greater the fear. How does this contribute to peace and happiness?

Allow me to walk you through a quick example: Let's say there was a product that would give me 6 percent growth, and I planned to retire in ten years. Let's say further that I know (by my own research) that 6 percent will give me a balance total capable of providing a relatively comfortable income for the later years of my life.

But then I get sidetracked. I hear about an incredible opportunity to earn 20 percent from a certain investment. That sounds much, much better than 6 percent! After all, I could live longer than expected. *And what if I don't have enough*? Yes, there's a risk involved, but I'm ready to take the risk in order to accumulate more. I hand over my money, expecting to see some big returns. I keep my money there, waiting for my lucky day. The year I expect to retire, I take a big hit, and it's all out the window. The money is lost.

By failing to take into account what I truly wanted in life (the peace of not having to worry about money), I chose instead to believe that only by high risks could I see high rewards. I forgot about all the other rewards coming my way from my other assets—my time with friends and loved ones, the memories, the home we have created. I was so focused on the accumulation of one asset—money—I took an unnecessary risk that in the end proved destructive to them all.

The entire *accumulation theory* presented in most retirement plans seldom produces peace and happiness because it focuses on one thing—stockpiling money. This is a measure focused on returns and not a measure of our objectives. Had the gentleman in our example stayed focused on his end objectives, or the "big picture" we talked about earlier, he would have had a secure retirement. Instead he was focused on the micro paradigm, the small picture, the accumulation of money now.

The desire to stockpile more than is needed has at its base *fear*. This is the *scarcity mentality* we talked about earlier, and at its root are all those feelings of *not having enough*—not enough money, not enough time—as evidenced in the example above by the gentleman who decided to go for the higher return. This mindset is debilitating. It shuts down creativity and bullies our dreams. When fear and greed rule the roost, our objectives are lost or forgotten and then become ultimately unattainable. In addition to the money that can be lost by investing this way, a person who is afraid of living longer than his savings will hold on to a job he doesn't enjoy for the sake of retirement benefits. And the saddest part is the lost opportunity. This person is essentially unproductive, forgoing his opportunity to create real value in the world around him.

MYTH #3: SELF-INSURING

The approach of risk transfer sits in exact opposition to self-insuring, much the same way that the old micro and the new macro are opposite paradigms. With self-insuring, we decide to pay for things as they come up. We hope that things work out and nothing catastrophic happens. We tell ourselves, "Oh, that will never happen to me." Or, "Those kinds of things don't happen to people like us." We convince ourselves that we are different or somehow "special." That there is no way we could ever lose our job, become disabled, or ultimately die. No, those things won't happen to us. And so we don't invest in an adequate health insurance plan, we don't plan for what will happen if the breadwinner of the household loses his job, and we certainly don't plan for what will happen in the event of death.

It might be easy to convince yourself that the tragedies of life will never happen to you, but the truth is they will happen to one degree or another. In a perfect world, they wouldn't. But even something as expected as the death of an elderly parent feels unexpected when you are the one who has to face it. If you prepare, if you follow the steps I will outline below, the unexpected loss may not be any less painful, but it will certainly be less stressful. Putting the foundation of risk transfer in place will protect you and your family from the unnecessary hardships that come when the unexpected happens, because in the end no one is left out. Death is something that happens to us all.

MAKING THE SHIFT: ACCUMULATION VS. UTILIZATION

What I am advising here ultimately comes down to a new way of looking at money. We need to shift our thinking completely from the old paradigm focused on accumulating money to the new paradigm focused on its utilization. This supports what we learned in the previous chapters: *money is a tool designed to serve.* It should never be given more importance than the people it was designed to help.

Making this shift will require awareness on your part because most of these paradigms were taught to us at an early age, and we have been living with them every day. The rest of the chapter will be focused on how to implement the idea of risk transfer in your own life with regard to your assets. At the end of the chapter, we will have several action exercises to help you make this important paradigm shift.

Below is a chart that gives insight into the difference between the theory of accumulation and utilization. Make a copy, write it down, or download it from our website for free at www.RichLife-ActionGuide.com. Post it in your workspace or where you normally pay your bills. I find it to be a good reminder and a useful tool for comparison.

ACCUMULATION	UTILIZATION
1. High Risk = High Return	1. Wise Risk = Safe Return
2. Self-Insure	2. Risk Transfer
3. Financial Products	3. Financial Strategies
4. Money Is the Asset	4. People Are the Asset

ACCUMULATION	UTILIZATION
5. Money Is Power	5. Wisdom Is Power
6. Behavior of Investment	6. Behavior of the Investor
7. Old Micro Paradigm	7. New Macro Paradigm
8. Stockbroker	8. RichLife Advisor

DO AS I SAY (NOT AS I DO)

We are now ready to talk about the nuts and bolts of risk transfer. As I mentioned earlier, successful financial institutions do not operate in the way that they advise their clients. I find this interesting. They expect you to trust them with your money on a regular, systematic basis. They want to hold onto your money for as long as possible—penalizing you if you want it back today—and if they lose any of it, well so be it. You expected there to be some loss at the get-go.

This begs the question: With regard to investing money, what are the banks and large companies doing? Well I'll tell you: they have set risk transfer strategies in place. They hire a Chief Risk Officer, or CRO, whose main job is to analyze risk to company assets and set policies in place to protect them. When a bank does a loan, what do they do? They check your credit, income, assets, and collateral, to transfer their risk. In other words, *they expect to make a profit*. And so to that end, they make sure they are covered. When banks started breaking their own rules and giving loans without first reducing their risk, the system collapsed.

All successful companies know the truth about money and risk: it's not the person who takes the most risk who wins. At the end of the day, it's the person who *transfers* the most risk that comes out on top.

We build our RichLife on the principle that money alone is not the key to a fulfilled life, and retirement is not the ultimate goal.

Living a fulfilled life is the goal. If you model what big corporations and banks do to build successful businesses, you will greatly increase your chances of living rich by reducing the amount of risk to your assets. This is the foundation to sound investing, because it's not about how much money you make, but how much you *keep*.

Transfer risk first—to your home, lifestyle, and all present and subsequent investments. This should be the first step and the first investment. Successful institutions do not even *begin* to address investment strategies until the appropriate foundation is in place to ensure their success. This is the bottom line for successful financial institutions, and it can be your bottom line as well. Build yourself a sound foundation *by transferring as much risk as possible.* You can do this by putting into place what I call the RichLife Security System.

RichLife Security System

In the same way that loan officers perform credit and asset checks, our team of RichLife Advisors have been trained that before we have a conversation about investments, we cover risk first. We set policies in place to make sure that what you have already built is covered and what you build next will be secured also. We are now going to talk about how you can do that by designing your own personal security system.

Remember those thieves we talked about at the beginning of this chapter? Stop and think for a moment why people spend a great deal of money on security systems for their homes. The answer is simple: with a good security system in place, the owner has peace of mind and can sleep at night. If not having to worry about money is the goal, then minimizing risk is the action you must take. In the same way a security system guards your home, a system can be put into place to guard your finances against what I call *the five thieves*.

No matter how much wealth you have accumulated and no matter the size of your net worth, these five thieves take you out of the game completely. I've seen it happen time and time again. Instances where a family had everything set up perfectly with regard to their financial investments and subsequent growth, but then suddenly the unexpected happened and they lost everything. In perfect world, we put these things in place and then never use them. Either way, you no longer have to worry about your money. Peace of mind will serve all areas of your RichLife once your security system is in place.

Let's go over each of the five thieves and see how disaster can be prevented in each case with various methods of *risk transfer*.

Thief #1: Market Loss

A few years after her daughter, Natasha, was born, my friend Diane bought a 529 plan for her college education. A 529 plan is a tax-deferred plan, similar to a 401(k) that allows you to save money for your children's college tuition. Diane continued contributing to the plan throughout Natasha's childhood, even when it wasn't easy. In fact, there were months when she had to lower her own standard of living to make that payment, but she still gave faithfully every month.

Just when her daughter was about to graduate high school, the market fell apart during the Great Recession of 2008. Natasha's college account suddenly dropped to half of its value at the moment when she needed it most. Diane had done everything right, but it didn't protect her daughter's future. Half of everything she had so carefully put aside for Natasha's college education was wiped out.

Market risk isn't just a problem for retirement accounts. It's a problem for anyone saving for a long-term goal. If the loss happens just prior to or during the time you are making the withdrawals, you won't have the opportunity to grow that money back.

As in the case of Diane in our story above, she had to withdraw money out of her account in the fall of the year her account value dropped by 50 percent. Not only did she lose money due to market loss, but her withdrawal compounded that loss, making it difficult to re-grow that money during the next four years.

With retirees, the danger of market loss during the years just prior to or just after retiring can have the same compounded negative effect. In fact, losing money during this time can greatly increase your chances of running out of money during your retirement years.

Most people aren't even aware of the risk their savings are exposed to until it's too late. The only way to protect against this thief is to *take proactive action*. You must prepare for this thief *before* he strikes. Afterward, it will simply be too late.

A good financial planner who understands your long-term and short-term goals can show you the areas where exposure to risk may not be in your best interest. Meeting regularly with your professional can also ensure that bad timing doesn't inadvertently wipe out your good intentions. Market investments are not bad, but because of their potential to lose money, they do need to be looked at more closely than other investments that are considered safe.

Thief #2: Taxes

Sahid was a single-parent father who had worked very hard to secure a future for his son. The boy's mother had died prematurely in a car accident, and Sahid was very diligent with the IRA account he set up for their future. He wanted to make sure his son would have full access to the funds if something unexpected happened to him. Though he wasn't what you would consider to be a wealthy man, at the time of his death, he had managed to build an IRA worth an impressive 1.2 million dollars.

What broke my heart, however, was what happened next.

The son, understandably in a state of shock and grief and without the guidance of an advisor, looked over the distribution options and checked the wrong box. He opted to receive his father's IRA in one lump sum because that was what made sense to him. The result? Eighty-one percent of the money ended up going to taxes. This was not what the father had intended. This was not what he had worked so hard for.

In this present economy, laws are changing, tax codes are changing, and the economy is changing—so much changes so fast that we don't know where tax rates will be a year from now. Because of this uncertainty, it makes sense to think about tax diversification. *Most people are familiar with the term "diversification" when it comes to their investment portfolios, but few people understand what this means with regard to their taxes.* Consider this: If you have 100 percent of your retirement savings in a 401(k), then 100 percent of your savings is taxable. That means when the time comes for you to retire and rely on that money for your income, you will be paying taxes on every penny that you withdraw. Not only that, but history shows us that tax rates only go up. Will you be taxed at a higher rate tomorrow than today? Chances are yes, which means it makes sense to take steps now to decrease your tax burden.

Tax diversification is a lot like diversifying your assets. It basically means giving yourself more than one option when it comes to paying the taxes on your lifetime of earned savings. Understanding the basics of tax diversification begins with a little bit of education about some basic terms associated with taxes. These terms relate to your investments—pre-tax, tax deferred, and tax-free.

Pre-tax Investments: While 401(k) plans and traditional IRAs are a great way to save, they are also a great way to build a big bucket of taxable money. The money sitting in these buckets hasn't been taxed yet. It will be taxed when you take the money out, either now or later.

Tax-deferred Investments: Some investments are taxed on their gains while they grow, while other investments are not. Investments that are allowed to grow without being taxed are called tax-deferred investments. The advantage to this is that they are able to take better advantage of compound interest, thus snowballing or accumulating growth more quickly. For example, a dollar that doubles annually and is allowed to grow *without tax* will grow to a sizable investment of $1,048,567 over the course of 20 years. That same dollar allowed to double but taxed at 28 percent annually will only grow to $51,353.

Tax-free Strategies: There are investment vehicles such as Roth IRAs and some life insurance products that allow for tax-free distribution. This means that when you take this money out at some future date, no taxes are owed. Yipee! It might make sense to roll over some of your money into one or more tax-advantaged investments. Traditional IRAs can be converted to Roth IRAs, giving you more control over when and how those taxes are paid.

Thief #3: Critical Illness

No one ever thinks there's a chance his or her life could be shattered by one of the Big Three—cancer, heart attack, and stroke. We all think, "That's not going to happen to me." Honestly, even though I know the statistics, I often think it won't happen to me, either.

Here's the hard truth: If you're married, statistics say that there's a good chance one of the Big Three will strike. The Centers for Disease Control and Prevention (CDC) reported in 2009 that 75 percent of people over 40 experienced a critical illness at some point during their lives. What you need to be prepared for is that surviving one of the Big Three could become your biggest problem. The number-one cause of bankruptcy in the U.S. is surviving a critical illness. When the rent or mortgage payments cannot be met, families face losing their homes. Relationships become strained and the quality of life becomes greatly compromised. Add to that the fact that medical bills continue to pile up and you have a real recipe for disaster. The accounts you have set up for other purposes such as college tuition and retirement become tapped. You would gladly spend all of it ten times over to insure the health and wellbeing of a loved one, but after all is said and done, where does this leave you and your family with regard to your RichLife?

If you don't plan for this thief, you're wide open to having your future destroyed. This is why planning for critical illness is part of a solid financial foundation. Without a contingency plan in place, just one major medical event could wipe out your entire future.

Thief #4: Cost of Long Term Care

Ted and Donna went in to see their financial advisor about restructuring their investment portfolio to support them during retirement. Ted was a retired naval officer in excellent health who still lifted weights and ran five miles a day, six days a week. He was only 65 years old when he retired, and he took offense when the advisor suggested they make plans for long-term care. "We don't need that!" Ted said. "We aren't the kind of people who need that. I'm in the prime of my life!"

Six months down the road, Ted was diagnosed with a rare lung disease that gradually made it more and more difficult for him to get around. He had to stop running as breathing became more diffi-cult. Because he refused to go to a nursing home, caring for Ted fell to his wife, Donna. As Ted became more and more incapacitated, Donna had to do more and more for him—things such as help-ing him in and out of the bathtub and feeding him. This changed the nature of their relationship. This wasn't at all what Donna had envisioned when she dreamed about their retirement years, and as Ted's illness progressed she became more and more emotionally and physically exhausted.

If you are near or entering retirement age, funding long-term care is one area you will also want to pay close attention to. Dis-ability affects 69 percent of people who live to be in their 90s, and the cost of proper care can quickly deplete your financial resources. Even if you are in excellent health now, it's important to consider the changes that might be coming down the road. According to the U.S. Department of Health and Human Services, 70 percent of 65-year-olds today will need some form of long term care, and 20 percent of those cases will require care for five years or longer.

Long-term care includes intrinsic nursing care at home, basic custodial services such as shopping or taking out the garbage, and care at an assisted living facility or nursing home. Medicare does not pay for extended services or chronic illness but rather is designed to pay for short-term medical conditions of six months or less that are expected to improve. Ted and Donna were not eligible for Medicare benefits because Ted's condition was chronic and not expected to improve. Not only did his condition deplete their assets, it depleted Donna's spirits. As more and more was asked of her, the quality of her RichLife suffered.

Today, there are many choices when it comes to protecting yourself against this thief. Many newer life insurance products offer critical care riders and living benefits to help cover the costs of long-term care. These are benefits you can access while you are still alive to help pay for the increasing costs of long-term care. You can use the money to pay for in-home care if you are more comfortable staying home, or you can use the money to help cover the cost of a nursing home or assisted living facility. Either way, with these life insurance products, if you are lucky enough to never need the care, the benefit is paid out to your beneficiaries.

Thief #5: Premature Death

My own father died at age forty-nine. He had a successful business, but that was of little use to my mother after he was gone. My father had been diligent to invest back into his retail nursery business, but he had omitted the simple step of purchasing enough life insurance. As a result, my mother's day-to-day life became much more difficult after he passed away. The grieving process is never easy for anybody. But had a substantial policy been in place, her financial stresses would have been greatly reduced. My dad worked very hard and had every intention of taking care of his family. None of us ever imagined he would die at such an early age, including him. We simply weren't prepared.

This is a scenario that I've seen repeated many times over in the lives of my clients. I urge you not to take this advice lightly. So many people have learned the hard way, but you don't have to. No one likes to think about dying. Because of this, many families are caught short when premature death does occur. Accidents, disease, or illnesses can take the breadwinner out of the picture and leave the survivors in a financially compromised position. We don't ever want to think about something like that happening, but death is the one thing in our lives that we can count on happening. No one is excluded. It only makes sense to be prepared.

No one is guaranteed a tomorrow. If you already have a life insurance policy set in place, I am happy to hear it. But it might be time to give that policy a check-up.

The incident that comes to mind involves a lady I met recently whose husband (the breadwinner) was killed in an accident. When the wife went to collect the life insurance, she learned that just the year before her husband's death, the policy had gone to *half its value*. The original policy itself would not have been sufficient, but half was almost a joke. It left her with no financial safety net. And again the hardship that resulted could easily have been prevented.

The message here is that it's not enough to have a policy in place. That policy must be reviewed on a regular basis to make sure the *security system* is in good working order. In the same way that you test the batteries on your smoke alarm, these policies must also be tested against the current situation. Life changes. You want the peace of mind knowing that if something happened to the income-earner, your family can keep their RichLife intact. That means updating those policies to reflect your current lifestyle.

I've lost count of the times that people have brought in policies to me that haven't been looked at in 10 to 20 years. Sadder still is the fact that most of the time clients do not even understand the *terms* of their policies. This goes back to raising your financial IQ. Do you remember practicing fire drills at school as a kid? Or even in your own home? Understanding your policies is the mental equivalent of a fire drill. You want to know both what is in place and what will be required of you should the unexpected happen. You want to know where the emergency exits are, and you want to know them well, so that in a time of panic or distress you can move through the steps with sure footing.

TERMITES: THE SNEAKY THIEVES

While the above thieves are the Big Five that can literally wipe out a lifetime of savings, there is a smaller group of thieves that can also do quite a bit of damage. I call these thieves *termites* because, although seemingly insignificant, they can eat away at your RichLife. *Sneaky termite thieves include fees to individual investment accounts, possible lawsuits, and future inflation.* Of the three, inflation is the most aggressive termite with a potentially devastating appetite.

The United States government has estimated the rate of inflation over a 10-year period between 2004 to 2014 to be between 2.5 and 3 percent. What this means to your buying power is that it gets reduced, or eaten, by that same three percent. Multiply that by the next ten years and you'll see that for every dollar you have saved, you really only have 70 cents. If you think about what you paid for your first house as compared to what you just paid for your last vehicle, you might get an idea of how powerful inflation can be.

While protection against the big thieves involve proactive steps, fighting against termite thieves is even trickier. It requires using multiple strategies and investment tools and the guidance of a financial professional who can analyze the durability of your current investments.

The bottom line: Thieves don't just eat away at your house and finances; they also eat away at your RichLife. A security system doesn't just protect your house; it protects everything we've been talking about.

FINAL WISHES

This is where having a team of reputable and qualified professionals comes into play. We will spend the next chapter talking about how to build your RichLife Team, but for the purposes of financial planning, it's important to understand that having a plan in place and a reliable professional who can help your family with that plan will greatly increase the odds that they are taken care of in the event of your death. This is the idea of risk transfer as applied to your family. Simply put, communicating your final wishes with someone capable of their execution protects your family from the unnecessary risk of thieves such as taxes and inflation. Most financial planners can help walk you through this as long as you spend some time on it first.

> Taking the time to set Final Wishes in place is a way to transfer risk for your family in case something happens to you.

I usually recommend that clients hold a family meeting with their kids so that everybody knows what's going on. That way, they know who I am and where they can go if they have questions or need help. I recommend they set up what I call *Final Wishes*. You can do the same thing on your own even if your financial planner does not offer these services.

In creating a legacy, you want your intentions honored. You want your family to know what those intentions are and who they can turn to for advice to be sure those intentions are carried out. Having a trusted professional prepared to do this will provide your loved ones with the guidance they need and you with peace of mind.

Setting up your final wishes basically involves something as simple as putting your thoughts on paper. What most people neglect is the next step of finding someone they trust who can communicate these intentions to those involved. Remember Sahid who worked so hard to build up a legacy for his son? Taking his father's IRA as a lump sum distribution was positively the worst choice the son could have made in that scenario. It is one of those irreversible money decisions that, once done, cannot be undone. But it can be prevented.

PORTFOLIO BUILDER

While wise investments are ones that a person steps into with a great deal of confidence, this requires study, research, and attention—and of course, wise *stewardship*. Adopting the paradigm shift from accumulation of money to utilization of money allows you to avoid the common investment mistakes made by the majority of individuals. With this mindset, you can make the shift from the micro-paradigm focused on stockpiling money and self-insuring, to the new macro paradigm that keeps the big picture—your goals and objectives—in mind.

Investing this way begins with the sound foundation of risk transfer. It doesn't matter if you have $10 million in perfect investments—if risk transfer strategies are not in place, every penny sits at risk. Assets such as your home and retirement are vulnerable to any one of *the five thieves*. Investing without a RichLife Security System in place is not only putting the cart before the horse, but allowing that cart to sit out in the open where it is vulnerable to catastrophe.

Why work your entire life to build up a net worth if you aren't going to take measures to protect it? It's a fairly simple matter to set up a risk transfer *security system* and to keep it in place at all times. Not only will this investment protect you and your family, but it will also buy you one of life's most priceless assets—the peace of mind that comes from planning.

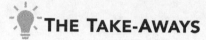 THE TAKE-AWAYS

- One of the best ways to decrease your risk is to increase your financial IQ.

- To increase your chances of winning, you must decrease your chances of losing.

- Not having to worry about money is what truly brings peace and happiness.

- A strong foundation of risk transfer is the secret to sound investing.

- Having a RichLife Security System in place will protect you against the five thieves that can steal your RichLife—market loss, taxes, critical illness, long-term care costs, and death.

ACTION STEPS

- **Know where you are:** Get out any policies that you currently have and take a look at them. These include life, home, health, and disability insurance. Many people have policies that have lapsed and don't even know it. Still others don't have the protection they need. Spend some time reviewing these to make sure they meet the needs of your situation today or, better yet, set up a review appointment with a professional. Many of our RichLife Advisors offer a free thirty-minute consultation review. It's a good rule of thumb to have these policies reviewed by a professional if it's been five years or more.

- **Identify any holes in your security system:** You can access a RichLife Security System Checklist online, or draft up your own checklist from the points made in this chapter. Designate a notebook or a separate folder for each of the five thieves, and give yourself 20 points for each thief you have covered. Most people find their security system to be operating at 20 percent. Make a list of what needs to be done to set the security system in place. For life insurance, for example, do you have a policy in place for each of the bread winners of your household? Is this policy term or whole? Is it appropriate for your current situation

- **Choose one area that needs some work:** Pick something that can be done, and give yourself an assignment. As with previous action steps, list how much and by when. For example: Call three life insurance providers and get a quote by the end of the week.

- **Properly allocate and diversify your assets:** It's vitally important for anyone within a 10-year window of their savings goal to take a close look at the amount of risk their investment is exposed to. Do you feel your portfolio is adequately diversified? If the market took a drop tomorrow, what percent of your assets would suffer a loss? Are you comfortable with that?

- **Write down your final wishes:** Review, update, or create a will, healthcare directive, and financial power of attorney. A will only goes into effect *after* you die and may not distribute your assets as you would wish. For guidance or answers to your questions, visit us at www.BeauHenderson.com.

- **Begin the process of searching for a financial professional.** It's important to have your current policies reviewed and updated, to make sure your listed beneficiaries are current, and to have a will or living trust put in place before one of the five thieves strikes. A qualified financial professional can help connect you with the professionals you need to accomplish all your objectives. Start with references from family and friends. Use the internet as a tool, and check out their profile and company information on sites such as LinkedIn.

- **Download your free copy of the Action Guide** for *The RichLife: Ten Investments for True Wealth* at www.RichLifeActionGuide.com.

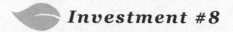 *Investment #8*

BUILD YOUR RICHLIFE TEAM

"If everyone is moving forward together,
then success takes care of itself."

—Henry Ford,
founder of the Ford Motor Company

A TEAM IN TANDEM

Several years ago when seeking advice for some real estate investments, I could not find an attorney and an accountant who would give me the same advice. The accountant talked from a tax standpoint while the attorney talked from a liability standpoint, and the advice they gave pointed me in two different directions. What I really wanted to know was what steps to take next, but their opinions left me directionless. Their advice reflected their respective professional points of view but left me frustrated and with no answers with regard to the one view that mattered most to me—*mine*.

I knew what I wanted to do, but I was unable to find the cohesive strategy I needed to make sure my bases were covered. After consulting with professionals in their respective fields, I was still left to figure it out on my own. So what was the point in seeking out professional advice? This dilemma set me about giving some serious thought to the necessity of building a team.

I began to imagine the benefits to clients that would occur if professionals worked together. In this ideal scenario, accountants, real estate agents, attorneys, and the like would comprise a team who not only worked for you, the client, but with each other. I imagined how they would convene and hold meetings so that advice and strategies were given to clients with the bigger picture in mind. The result of a coordinated strategy all across the board would cover all areas of a person's life, resulting in the best possible outcomes specifically tailored for the individual client. This team of advisors would not only know one another but network together, supporting their mutual clients and increasing their respective business. They would become a team of professionals whose goal and reputation was to offer the best possible service to their clients. This was the birth of RichLife Advisors, and it has now become more than just an imagined reality

RICHLIFE ADVISORS

Do you remember the son we talked about in the previous chapter who lost 81 percent of his father's IRA? The son may have acted without the guidance of a financial advisor, but what if the attorney he met with *knew* the financial advisor who set up the IRA? That attorney could have picked up the phone himself and called the financial advisor to set up an appointment for the son to discuss his distribution options. That one extra step could have saved the boy hundreds of thousands of dollars. Imagine what he could have done with that money.

Irreversible money mistakes
can be prevented if you have a
team of advisors in place.

When professionals keep to their chosen niche, they operate for the most part in a vacuum. When professionals work together, they have a greater ability to offer advice consistent with your goals. Ideally, this team will cover the bases of all your assets and include professionals such as a real estate agents, accountants, financial planners, attorneys, personal trainers, and coaches. If they are all onboard and aware of your intentions, they will be able to confer together. Think of how that could work to your advantage when strategizing and coordinating your life. It's your responsibility to build your RichLife team, and this is what I teach my clients to do. The team will work for you if you set it up that way. If you take an active approach to selecting your professionals, the care you receive and the quality of service will be higher.

Building a team won't happen overnight. I've been working on building mine for the last ten years now. At times some professionals have been upgraded or replaced for a better fit as the team continues to grow. I rely on the professionals in my team. My own goal is to build a team that works well together to serve both my clients and myself. Because of my profession, I am part of the team I'm helping to build. You might find this to be true for yourself as well, depending on your professional situation. Either way, you'll discover that working with this end goal in mind results in both personal and professional gains. I have found that any steps taken toward this aim result in improved outcomes, both personally and professionally, regardless of how far you get in creating the ideal.

The reason for these improved results is because by definition, RichLife Advisors are those professionals who are at the top of their field. They are some of the best at what they do, well respected, and well thought of by fellow colleagues and clients. The reason for their success is simple: They have chosen to adapt and follow the RichLife principles set forth in this book. These professionals are doing the work they do because they have identified it to be a main area of their life purpose. Whether you are a client seeking their services or a professional seeking a networking partner, these are the individuals you want to work with.

If you would like to know how to identify and build a team of professionals who work *for* you, please, read on.

SELECT PROFESSIONALS WITH CARE

If you had a serious medical problem and needed care, would you choose a doctor who handled his practice on a part-time basis, as a kind of hobby? Or one who had few, if any, references and no real record of successful surgeries? If it was your child who required medical attention, who would you want to perform their surgery? To provide their follow-up care? You would want only the best.

I realize these may sound like silly questions, but often I see people choosing their team of professionals in just such a lackadaisical manner. Their accountant may be a family friend. Their real estate agent might be the neighbor down the street who just happened to get his license a few years ago. And on it goes. This results in a team of individuals who may know you, but who may not be the best team to help move you toward your RichLife.

Choosing professionals simply because we like them and we know them is a basic human instinct. We reason that if they know who we are, they will care about us and give us better service. In some cases, they may not be capable of giving the best service in their chosen industry. This is fine when we are talking about lawn mowing or other such services, but with regard to you and your family's financial future, I suggest that you go with the best team possible. Subscribing to the RichLife philosophy when building your team allows you to have your cake and eat it too. Not only will these professionals take the time to get to know you, but they will be more knowledgeable and more skilled at what they do than the average Joe because, as I mentioned before, it is their field of life purpose. They will also be well connected and able to lead you to other high-integrity professionals in other areas. The question is how do you find these people?

RAISING YOUR IQ

I have a colleague, LaShonda, who has started to look forward to her dental visits, not because she found a great doctor, but because the dental hygienist who works there is so passionate and knowledgeable about teeth, every time she goes in she learns something new. The hygienist's name is Katherine, and not only does she clean your teeth, she *explains* them to you. She tells you what to watch out for, how to counter the bad habits you've developed such as sipping all day on lattes or soda pop. She listens to your concerns and freely volunteers information. "I've never seen someone so excited about teeth," LaShonda remarks. "For the first time in my life, I understand the function of dental floss and so now I'm flossing. No one ever explained it to me before. It's not just about the food that's stuck between your teeth!"

LaShonda has found a professional with high integrity and knowledge. Katherine isn't teaching people about teeth because she gets a financial bonus or reward for doing so at the end of her day. She does it because she can't help herself. Her sincere passion on the subject of teeth propels her to the highest levels of integrity and service because she wants to share this knowledge with her patients. She cares. It's important to note here what Katherine is doing—*she is raising the dental IQ of her patients.*

Corey Jahnke is a pharmacist who doesn't just hand out prescriptions and say, "Don't take this on an empty stomach." He takes time to get to know his customers. He treats them as if they were his friends. He asks them, "How did the softball game go?" Or, "How's that sprained ankle?" These interactions add to his RichLife because they take away the monotony of his day, develop new relationships, and give him enjoyable experiences. His customers in turn benefit from his sincerity and professional knowledge.

We have all been told that you should trust your doctor and other healthcare providers. We've also been told the same thing about financial planners. What I'm suggesting, however, is that these professionals earn your trust first, before you give it away. What you are looking for here are people like Katherine and Corey, people who offer you not only service, but who seek to raise your level of knowledge and develop relationships. This is the secret:

> Give your trust to those professionals who raise your IQ within their given field of study while offering you their service or care.

This goes back again to the idea of stewardship, because at the end of the day, you are the one responsible for your health, your money, the condition of your teeth. You are the one who must take action with regard to any advice given by a professional. If you know *why* you are doing it and to what aim, you will be much more likely to succeed.

I appreciate that my clients trust me, but more than that I want them to understand what they're doing and why they're doing it. If you understand something, you're actually gaining wisdom you can build on for the rest of your life. But if you're just doing what I tell you to do for twenty years and then I go away, you won't have grown at all. It is my goal that we work together, co-creating a sound financial future. It is my hope that after working with me, you become a better investor. Things that were risky before are now wise decisions because your financial IQ has been raised.

EDUCATION AND ENTHUSIASM

Once someone has identified their life purpose, what is it that sets them apart from other professionals? Sussil Liyanage in Sri Lanka identified his life purpose in the field of financial services, but he took his profession to a new level. He achieved the quality of a RichLife by combining his life purpose with a passion. There are two main elements that come into play here with regard to people who follow the RichLife principles, either consciously or otherwise.

People who have found the work they love to do can't help but excel because they are naturally driven to educate themselves in regard to their field. Our dental hygienist Katherine still attends regular dental conventions, not because she has to, but because she wants to keep up with the latest developments in her field. Corey the pharmacist has taken what he's learned from serving his customers to create a book of parables called, *Show Up and You're Half-way There*. These professionals have an innate thirst for knowledge and are constantly striving to improve both their own lives and the lives of others. They read books, take classes, listen to interviews. As professionals, they have more than just a job, they have a mission.

Corey Jahnke explains, *"Successful people are somewhat irrational. They pick a goal that means so much to them, they get up early and stay up late.* They also invest in themselves. To quote the very successful motivational speaker, Brian Tracy, 'Successful people invest 10 percent of their income in themselves.' This means they buy the book, they listen to the CD, they go to the seminars, and they do the training. Most people think, *I can't afford to do that.* The truth is, you can't afford not to! I learned this myself after investing in a seminar led by Darren Hardy, the publisher of *Success* magazine. The seminar cost me $2,000, and I've made that back 10 times over because of what he taught me. Getting that education put me light years ahead of where I was before."

Professionals who have found their life purpose in their given field will continually be educating themselves and then sharing what they learn with those they serve. Even someone who is relatively new to their chosen field will have an *"I can find out!"* attitude with regard to any question you could ask them. What they lack in experience they make up for in enthusiasm, which means you don't need to worry about being in the hands of a rookie who is working in the area of their life purpose. Rest assured they will do whatever it takes and then some to insure your satisfaction because they love what they do.

But this is only the beginning of what propels them to greater success.

THE POINT OF VIEW OF COWS

While earning her Masters of Science at Arizona State University, Temple Grandin became fascinated with the behavior of cattle. Specifically, she wanted to know what caused them to moo. At first she was ridiculed for her question; after all, cows moo and geese honk and what's to be done about that? But she was convinced that the cows were communicating to one another due to the tremendous stress of their environment. New arrivals to any typical cattle ranch are first led through what they call a flea-dip, where the animal is fully submerged into a water bath to rid the creature of parasites. Because of the cow's fear and agitation, drowning was a common occurrence, resulting in several unnecessary deaths a week. This was bad for profits and bad for the cow.

Temple believed it was not only possible to do better, but necessary. She believed that as stewards to these animals who would in turn provide us with nourishment, we *owed* them a measure of respect. She spent months researching and observing the behavior of cows, visiting livestock auctions, ranches, and slaughterhouses. But she didn't just observe. She got down on her hands and knees and looked through the chutes. She saw things from the point of view of the cows.

Ms. Grandin has Asperger's Syndrome, and as a scientist, she realized that animals and autistics share similar traits—they both rely on visual clues to navigate their surroundings. Because she saw things the way they did, she was able to understand what distressed them. These were easily overlooked things such as shadows and contrasting light, shiny objects or clothing draped over fence rails. She also understood what calmed them. Because of this unique perspective, she was able to design and develop a flea-dip that cattle willingly walked into. The cows followed a solid-walled curve into a chute that squeezed them and kept them subdued. There was no mooing and no balking. They walked quietly and with sure footing down onto the final ramp and right into the water. The entire design was considered nothing less than genius.

UNDERSTANDING WIN/WIN

Temple Grandin is now one of the most respected names in her field. An associate professor of Animal Science, the author of several books, and the recipient of numerous awards, half of all slaughterhouses in the United States employ her designs and innovations. The result is a win/win for both the company and the cows. By respecting the fears and sensitivities of the animals, there are fewer accidents and deaths, higher profit margins for the companies, and better quality meat for consumers.

In the national bestseller classic, *The 7 Habits of Highly Effective People*, Stephen Covey devotes an entire chapter to the philosophy of win/win. He describes this paradigm as the Third Alternative and writes: "It's not your way or my way; it's a better way, a higher way." The paradigm is based on the belief that one person's success does not need to be achieved at the expense of another's.

Professionals such as Temple Grandin who are at the top of their field are there not just because of their skill sets. They have succeeded because they know the secret to building a RichLife: always operate with the client's best interest in mind.

Though she was not hired by them, the clients in Temple Grandin's case were the cows. The owners of the slaughterhouses were not operating with the cows' best interests in mind; they were simply trying to move as many of them through the chute as possible. But she was able to show them that what was good for the cows was also good for them. With regard to professionals in any industry, whether it is cattle farming or financial planning, those at the top of their field know this secret to good business: *what's good for their clients is also good for them.*

In the last chapter we talked about the mistake inherent in the myth *high risk equals high return.* What we are talking about now is another one of those erroneous memes we've all come across: *in order for somebody to win, somebody has to lose.* A RichLife Advisor knows that if they are invested in helping their clients win, they win. We have a new equation here, one that takes the pressure off you always having to "win the game." When you understand that what is good for them is also good for you, the "game" becomes unnecessary and work becomes enjoyable.

You want to find professionals who live by this paradigm and have the ability to see things from your point of view. Professionals who seek first to understand where you are coming from, and second to add value. These professionals will begin with you first, seeking to understand your life situation and objectives. They will then seek to add value by offering their skills or services to further your objectives. If what they do cannot help you achieve your goals, they will recommend the help or services of someone who can. It's that simple. There is no game to play, no *I win or you lose.* It's about a partnership, a co-creation, using the skills of the professional and the goals of you, the client.

IT'S ALL ABOUT YOU, BABY!

Let's say you are looking for a financial planner. You call around and set up a meeting. On the given day you arrive and are offered a cup of coffee or tea. You sit down in their office, feeling comfortable, and after a bit of chit-chat about the weather they ask to take a look at your financial statements. "Great," you say. "I have them right here."

Handing them over, you feel a little vulnerable, but realize this is a step you must take in order to get to where you want to go. The financial planner shuffles through the papers, taking a look at your accounts, nodding and saying things such as, "I see you have a Roth IRA set up. And a money market savings account." You also nod, about to ask a question when he sets down the papers and starts talking.

"You know, I've got this great new mutual fund that just came on the market last week. I've got a few clients in on it, and I'm doing it myself...." He goes on to talk about this great new product. He shows you brochures and spreadsheets. He compares its performance with those of other products. He spends twenty minutes of a thirty-minute meeting talking about this new product and you nod and ask questions, trying to understand. But something feels off.

These kinds of meetings happen every day. People are looking for advice and they set aside some time in their day to talk to a professional, but when they get there they don't get to talk. The professionals does all the talking, using terms and jargon their new client doesn't yet understand. Warning bells should go off in your head during meetings like these. What I tell my clients to do if they find themselves in a meeting like this is run.

It's *your* money and *your* future. The first meeting should be about *you*. Not about the mutual funds or products he or she may have to offer. And it shouldn't be about them, either. A professional who is working to impress you with their credentials and testimonies is another warning sign. The purpose of the initial meeting is to establish what your needs are and where you are headed. *If they don't start with your needs first, how can they know if they are helping you or not?* The answer is they can't. It might be the greatest mutual fund in the world, but that doesn't mean it's what you should be signing up for right now.

Think of it another way: if you go into a restaurant for dinner, your server knows one thing about you—he knows you are hungry. But that's all he knows. It would be impertinent of him to go ahead and order you a steak dinner without speaking to you first. It might be the greatest steak dinner in the entire world, but what if you're a vegetarian? That steak would be absolutely useless to you.

As funny as it may be to think about, you should go into any first meeting knowing *it's all about me.* If it's not, something is wrong. Understand this and you've taken the first step toward learning the difference between those professionals who have your best interests at heart and those who don't. The first are those you can trust and whom you want to do business with. The latter are simply trying to make a sale.

TRANSACTIONAL VERSUS RELATIONAL

There is a difference between selling for profit's sake and selling to meet the client's needs. Once you are aware of this important distinction, you will be able to select professionals with greater care. We all know that professionals must make a living, but the individual who is living her life purpose in accord with the RichLife philosophy will always operate in a way that leads to the higher good of everyone involved. What's best for their clients is also best for them; the needed income will follow.

In the world of business, relationships are often ignored. We've all heard the saying, "it's just business," which often translates as: "I don't have to consider what would be good for you." It is common for salespersons or business owners to look directly past the person they are doing business with to the money that is behind them, or, more accurately, in their wallets. But here's another tenet to keep in mind: Successful people understand that it's the person, not the money, who is the asset.

Clients who are treated well will come back. Clients who get exactly what they need will tell others. If someone recommends a professional in this way, take that as a good sign. Make the appointment and see how that first meeting goes. If they are good, they will *take the time to get to know you*. This, combined with their innate interest and knowledge in their given field, will give you the best possible service. In the end, you will benefit not just from their expertise, but from the knowledge they in turn pass on to you. When it comes to financial planning and the care of your assets, the result is greater peace of mind for you and your family.

As you begin to build your team, you want to look for professionals who operate by these tenets and who are able to adopt their client's point of view *before* giving advice. When attending meetings and interviews, ask yourself the following:

- Does the advisor listen and communicate in terms of helping you move toward your RichLife?

- Do they often refer back to the goals, dreams, and objectives that are important to you?

- Do they ask about *you first* before talking about themselves, their products, or services?

- Do they treat you as a person rather than as a sale?

- Do they share information with you, explaining the reasoning behind their advice in an effort to help raise your IQ?

- Are they honest with you?

PERSUASION VERSUS MANIPULATION

As a professional or a spouse or anyone in an important relationship, how do you make the switch from being transactional to relational? How do you make sure your customers and clients and husbands and wives feel valued? One of the most important things to understand when striving to provide this kind of high-level service and authenticity has to do with the difference between persuasion and manipulation. Bob Burg, author of *The Go-Giver* and *The Art of Persuasion: Winning Without Intimidation*, says that it comes down to understanding the difference between persuasion and manipulation. In talking with Bob about this important distinction, he had the following observations to share:

> Persuasion is a cousin of influence. It is the ability to move a person toward action with the desire of a specific goal. A lot of people have asked me, how is this different from manipulation? And I've given it a lot of thought. *The key difference is that persuasion allows both parties to improve their lives.*

In his book, *The Art of Talking So People Will Listen,* Dr. Paul Swets provides an outstanding explanation of the difference between persuasion and manipulation. He writes, "Manipulation aims at control, not cooperation. It results in a win/lose situation. It does not consider the good of the other party. Persuasion is just the opposite. The persuader seeks to enhance the self-esteem of the other party. The result is that people respond better because they are treated as responsible, self-directing individuals."

Think of manipulation and persuasion as being good and evil cousins. They are both concerned with the learned art of understanding human interaction. One uses skills to help others, the other uses their skills to help themselves.

Bob concludes: "Manipulators are so focused on themselves and their own self-interest; they do only what they feel is to their own benefit. And if it hurts the other person, so be it. What they don't realize is that not only is this not a good life practice, it's not good business practice."

Take a look at the following comparison chart to understand why:

MANIPULATORS	PERSUADERS
Have employees	Have loyal teams
Have customers	Have repeat business and referrals
Have family and friends	Have fulfilling relationships

For example, if I'm talking to you about your financial portfolio and I am trying to get you to consider a product, there is a difference between selling the product because I want the commission fee and selling because I think it's in your best interest and can help improve your situation.

Persuaders think only win/win. If it is not in the client's best interest, they don't try to sell it to them. The mentality here is always one of service. Selling this way begins with asking the right questions, understanding the customer's point of view, and figuring out how you can add value to their life by meeting their needs.

The question in your mind now might be, what about making money? Yes, treating people well can increase profits. Law number three of Bob Burg's *Go-Giver* addresses profit this way: "Your profits are determined by how abundantly you place other people's interests first." When your efforts are focused on doing what it is in the best interest of others, you work to create value for them.

If value is lightning, then money is the thunder. The commission or fee is the direct and natural result of the value that you provide. To quote motivational speaker Jim Rohn, "You don't get paid for the hour. You get paid for the value you bring to the hour."

VALUE TIMES TWO: JIM ROHN AND KYLE WILSON

The name Jim Rohn may be familiar to you. He was perhaps one of the world's most beloved motivational speakers, an American entrepreneur and author who moved millions not just because of what he taught, but because of how he made people feel. Jim's leadership wisdom and business coaching was distilled into 17 different books and audio/video programs; in 1985 he was the recipient of the National Speakers Association Council of Peers Award for excellence in speaking; his seminar career spanned a period of 39 years during which he shared his message with more than 6,000 audiences and over five million people.

You can do a Google search for Jim Rohn and read about how he achieved this success, but one name that won't likely come up on page one of the search is promoter and author Kyle Wilson. As founder of Jim Rohn International and Your Success Store, it was Kyle who built the platform to elevate Jim Rohn. His story of their partnership speaks directly to the power of connecting, building a team, and adding value.

"The two of us were able to take what we were doing and exponentially bring it to the next level," reflects Kyle during our 2014 interview. "I saw Jim speak onstage back in 1993. At the time I was a seminar promoter doing events all over the country, and when I heard him in front of an audience, I thought he was the best speaker in the world."

That night, Kyle made Jim an offer he couldn't refuse. It was an offer scribbled out on a cocktail napkin and a deal sealed with a handshake. That deal launched a ten-year working relationship that resulted in explosive success. Kyle took Jim's speaking gifts combined with his promoting skills to increase their opportunities, revenue, and status. Jim went from doing 25 gigs a year at a speaking fee of $4,000, to 110 speaking gigs annually with a fee of $10,000 and upward. Kyle literally reinvented the wheel to create a product line over the Internet that during the course of the next several years built the online presence of Jim Rohn to over one million plus subscribers. All of this due to the power of collaboration.

You might be wondering what the offer was that Jim couldn't refuse. I was curious myself, and so I asked Kyle during our interview. He explained: "It was true that Jim was taking more of a chance on me than I was on him, but it was also true that at the time, he didn't have anything. No list, no employers, and no team. He had lost a good deal of money on the previous three partnerships that he'd entered into, and so when I made Jim an offer that night, I agreed to assume all the risk. Instead of splitting everything 50/50, I paid for all the costs—the employees, the office, everything. I also paid Jim a percentage of everything. In this arrangement, we were less like partners and I was more like a publisher."

Kyle reinvented the terms of partnership to create not just a working relationship, but a legacy. It worked because they shared a common philosophy. Kyle sums it up: "Our core philosophy was always to bring value to each other. As long as we kept bringing so much value to one another, why would we want to work with anyone else?"

MISSION-DRIVEN BEINGS

Whether you are looking for a professional to collaborate with or a professional to help you with your specific needs, chances are you will instinctively pick up on things you might not know how to explain. These signals or cues are what allowed Jim and Kyle to launch a million-dollar business relationship using a cocktail napkin contract and handshake signature.

Ask yourself, how do you know that someone is honest? Sometimes it's a transparent statement such as, "I don't think that product would be a good fit for you," when you know this product would result in a huge sales commission for them. Other times it's a feeling you get, and a quality that is somehow in the conversation.

Steve D'Annunzio, a behavior modification teacher who mentors life success coaches all over the country, including the author of this book, conducted a ten-year study that revealed the different modes of being that people operate from in both life and business. D'Annunzio's work sheds light on the science of ontology, or the study of being, and points to the fact that people respond to what you are being even more than to what you are saying.

This explains why sometimes you "get a feeling" for someone without really knowing that much about them. This applies to choosing your professionals because ideally, you are looking for those who are "mission driven." Let's take a look at what that means. Listed below are four modes of being:

- **Fear Driven:** Marked by low production, low happiness, and a stubborn refusal to change. These people blame others, look outside for everything, and have a difficult time with self-reflection. The mode they operate from is one of getting and not giving. They see the world as a battlefield. Someone must lose in order for them to win, and everything is a fight. Life is a war. The language they typically use begins with "I can't," and the reasons place the blame on other people and forces not in their control.

- **Desire Driven:** These people experience average productivity and happiness. Aware they can do better, but having no idea how, these people are often self-sabotaging, eliminating any possibility of failure by disrupting opportunities to take chances, change, and succeed. They are always focused on the next thing, always wanting more. As a result, any success they do have is almost immediately drained of joy. They see the world as a trap. Always waiting for the other shoe to drop and invested in negative sayings such as "the worst thing that can happen will and at the worst possible time." The language of the desire driven often begins with "I want."

- **Pride Driven:** This is a tricky mode. Pride driven people are intelligent, high producers, giving them the appearance of success, but their happiness is tied to money, and so they are always insecure and incomplete. As a result, these people are controlling, insist on being seen as right, and they have variable integrity. They'll do what's in their client or customer's best interest some of the time, but only when it benefits them. They analyze each move like a chess game, and view life as a giant chessboard. Many of the world's most successful people operate from this mode, but their success is due to the manipulation of others to get what they want, much like moving pawns. They feel a sense of entitlement, often speaking the language of "I need" and so can justify breaking the rules. In order to move to the next mode, the win/win paradigm must be embraced.

- **Mission Driven:** Integrity is key for these people, and theirs is high. They're committed to excellence, intelligent, and productive, but their lives are also marked by balance: they achieve business and financial success at the same time as family joy and personal health. We've seen examples of these individuals throughout the book, including the true stories of Sussil Liyanage, Corey Jahnke, Jim Rohn, and Kyle Wilson. Because they all experienced the lower modes of being, they were able to give others the benefit of the doubt. They view life as a school, where challenging relationships or situations are opportunities to learn instead of threatening situations. They are so focused on what they can give and do to help others that fear of failure or not getting back no longer enters into the equation. In this mode, their language transforms as follows:

- "I can't" *becomes* "How can I?"
- "It's not my fault" *becomes* "I'm responsible."
- "It's a problem" *becomes* "It's an opportunity."
- "I wish" *becomes* "I know."
- "If only" *becomes* "Next time."
- "What will I do?" *becomes* "I'll handle it!"
- "How awful!" *becomes* "What's the lesson?"
- "I need" *becomes* "I create."
- "I want" *becomes* "I choose."

  (Courtesy of Soul Purpose Institute ©2006)

Finding mission-driven professionals is obviously your goal because these are the people capable of providing the best service to you, your family, and friends. They also make for synergistic collaborations such as the case with Jim Rohn and Kyle Wilson. According to D'Annunzio's research, about one third of all professionals you meet are mission driven, while the majority of people operate from one of the three lower modes. Have you seen these people? Are you working with any of them now? Do you recognize yourself in any of these different modes?

As a side note with regard to your life purpose, you also want to *become* someone whom others will seek out as well. You want to identify your own mode of being so you can move up, attain higher levels of success and prosperity, and ultimately achieve your RichLife. I currently coach a program with Steve called the Mission Driven Advisor or MDA program. This class works with professionals to further illuminate their modes of being and help them to learn what they can do differently in order to shift up. This class makes up part of the curriculum for those who want to become RichLife Advisors.

By learning to identify these modes of being in others, you can begin to build your team of professionals. By learning to identify your own mode of being, you can begin to achieve the kind of professional success you see in those whom you admire.

A Note on Outsourcing

As a working professional, there are many areas of my work where I outsource projects. I do this because I value my time and am not looking to become an expert in every field. If it is an area in which I have zero interest, I take the time to find and hire someone who *is* interested. The results are always better than what I could have done myself, because when I outsource, I'm looking for the candidate who is mission driven and living out his or her life purpose.

For instance, when I need someone to work with me on technical projects—anything from social media to developing with my website—I outsource. I don't know anything about it and don't *want* to know anything about it. I'm not a tech-type of a guy and I know it. When interviewing professionals, I need an individual (or individuals) who not only understand my objectives but who *care* about my objectives and are able to explain things to me in a way that I can understand.

By the way, this is another great clue to your life purpose. It's as much about knowing what you are not good at and what you dislike doing as it is about discovering what you love to do.

If there are aspects to your line of work that you find distressing, it might be time to take a look at outsourcing those projects. If you often give public speeches for example, but loathe the effort of sitting in front of a computer, banging out the right words, hire a freelance writer to find the perfect words for you. By outsourcing on a per-project basis, you can support the life purpose of others and achieve better results for yourself. It's another example of win/win. Remember, your time and energy are assets. Why waste precious energy on projects you aren't suited for if you don't have to?

We have been taught all of our life that we should strengthen our weak areas. But as a working adult, I've found that the most successful people stay in the areas they are strongest in and work instead to build a team that complements the areas outside their purpose. They outsource and work within an interdependent business model where strategic partnerships are created and talents combined. This allows greater leverage for both success and money.

PORTFOLIO BUILDER

At the beginning of this chapter, I brought up the idea of a team of professionals who knew each other and worked together for the best interests of the clients. This is what I have developed over the years with RichLife. We are training advisors and attracting team members—professionals from all over the world who subscribe to the RichLife philosophy. These are people who are top in their field because they are living out their life purpose with passion and they want what is best for you. Their success is built on and dependent upon the success and wellbeing of their clients. You can find them at BeauHenderson.com.

You can also begin building your own RichLife team of professionals. The responsibility of team building is 100 percent up to you and starts with whatever professionals you need. For almost everyone it will involve an accountant and an attorney. Additionally it might include your real estate agent, insurance agent, financial planner, and personal trainer or life coach. Your collaboration might also include a professional working relationship with someone who balances your weaknesses with their strengths. Collaborating with professionals like these can also exponentially increase and optimize your own professional success.

When interviewing professionals, listen to what they say and the order in which they say it. Ascertain whether or not they have your best interests at heart. Professionals living in the RichLife paradigm will be mission-driven beings, dedicated to serving their clients by doing what they enjoy.

THE TAKE-AWAYS

Irreversible money mistakes can be prevented if you have the right team of advisors in place.

- RichLife Advisors are those professionals who are at the top of their field because they have identified the work they do to be their life purpose.

- Give your trust to those professionals who raise your IQ within their given field while offering you their best service or care.

- Successful professionals always operate with the client's best interests in mind. They seek first to understand where you are coming from, and second to add value.

- Your influence and financial success is determined by how abundantly you place other people's interests first.

- Mission-driven beings will treat their clients as valued relationships and not as transactions.

 ## ACTION STEPS

- Make a list of professionals you would like to build for your team. Be sure to include a financial advisor, tax accountant, and a lawyer. If you already have those positions filled, write in their names.

- Take a look at your "team" members. Evaluate which level of being they operate from and ask yourself if there are any members who need to be released in order to help move you closer to your RichLife.

- Start filling in your "open" spots by setting up appointments and meetings. Bring along a checklist to remind yourself, *it's all about me*, and write down your impressions of what they are "being."

- You can start building your "professional" team by making a list of both your strengths and weaknesses. List those parts of your job that you do not enjoy. If any task falls in an area of your "weakness" then consider outsourcing.

- **Bonus Gift**: Download your free copy of the Action Guide for *The RichLife: Ten Investments for True Wealth* at www.RichLifeActionGuide.com.

 *Investment #9*

PROTECT YOUR PRIMARY ASSET

"The greatest wealth is health."

—Virgil, Roman poet

YOU AND YOUR HEALTH

Rule number one of Cherie Carter-Scott's book, *If Life Is a Game, These Are the Rules*, states: "You will be given a body." You can't play the game of life without it. Like it or hate it, love it or ignore it, this is your vehicle for the duration of your time here on earth. This body will serve to transport you through life.

We only get one body. There are no backups or used models available. You might find it necessary to replace certain parts—modern medicine has now made this possible. But once the body has been broken beyond repair, the game of life is over. We know this. Yet most of us live as if pretending our bodies didn't exist.

I have a friend, Rick Almand, who often reminds me, "Take care of that primary asset!" He isn't talking about my mutual funds. He's talking about my health. Rick has realized the importance of good health and makes it a point to ask the question: "Without your health, how can you enjoy what you have accomplished? How can you take advantage of all that you've gained?"

The answer is you can't. It doesn't matter if you have millions in the bank, without good health you simply won't enjoy it. Simple activities, trips, or other adventures become painful. If you have trouble with breathing or walking or any other type of physical exertion, time with loved ones becomes compromised. You might choose to push through the pain or medicate it, but even that will only take you so far. And the medical bills that a person can run into by neglecting their health often approach such astronomical figures that retirement savings can be wiped out. Now this is a dire picture to paint. But let me assure you, it's much better to think about all this now rather than wait until it's too late to change anything.

You have a body. Your health is an asset—one of the most easily overlooked and most often ignored—but an asset nonetheless. In this chapter, we are going to move it back up to the number-one spot where it belongs.

LIFESTYLES OF THE DRIVEN AND AMBITIOUS

We see it portrayed on prime time every night: Nicely dressed professional comes rushing down the stairs, ignores the offer of breakfast, and heads out the door. Or how about: Nicely dressed professional stays up all night working on a case, falls asleep at desk, and wakes up next morning in the office. Nicely dressed professional has a busy day, goes out to a bar, has too much to drink...I could go on and on. We watch these shows because they mirror our own lives, or the lives we hope to have. They depict the lifestyles of successful professionals, the lifestyles we hope to create for ourselves.

Or do we?

The lifestyles of the very driven tend to be rich in poor habits. Lack of sleep, lack of exercise, and too much processed foods are the norm. The job is given priority, not the person. Stress levels are high and anxiety an everyday occurrence, with no time for breaks or physical exercise. You can maintain this kind of regimen for a while, and it does look pretty sexy on TV. But in reality, this kind of a lifestyle is unsustainable. Your body is robbed of its health and vitality. Severe and life-changing consequences are the result. They show that on TV, too, but in real life it's not at all fun and the ending disappoints.

I say this tongue in cheek, but it's a serious subject. This idealized lifestyle has become almost standard fare for the brightest and most driven among us. These are the people so focused on building a business, a career, or climbing that corporate ladder he or she fails to be a good steward to their health. The desire for money and success becomes paramount at the risk of personal health. Medical experts tell us that the high-achiever, A-personality types often expose themselves to greater health risks because they are competitive, driven, and most likely to push themselves to the extreme. They do whatever it takes to get the job done, ignoring the physical signs that something is wrong, or medicating those symptoms so they can keep going.

Statistics show that these people are the most prone to having coronary heart disease, elevated blood pressure, and blood clotting. Common sense tells you their bodies are only fighting back.

HEALTH ALERTS!

If you have come this far through the book, by now you have seen through the fairy tale that tells you money alone brings contentment and peace. Building a RichLife is a holistic approach that extends to and includes all facets of your life. Physical health, peace of mind, and a general sense of fulfillment sit at the top of the list. When you have a sound body, the rest of you is free to perform at its best.

The good news here is that you don't have to punish your body in order to achieve success.

It is possible to take care of your health and get the job done, both. In fact, taking care of yourself ultimately results in more effective, efficient doing.

The experience of fatigue, pain, or discomfort is your body's built-in security system. This is how it tells you that something is wrong. If the alarm goes off on your home security system, you wouldn't ignore it, put ear protectors on, and continue to go about your business. No! You would address the problem. If a window has been broken, you would take the time to get it repaired. It might simply be that the security code needs to be reset. Oftentimes, the body needs to "reset" also, and we will talk about that later. Alarms also signal the presence of an intruder.

It has become common practice in the work place for employees who are sick to show up for work anyway. Sometimes this is a personal decision based on money, other times it is a necessity—there is simply no one else to take their place. Striving for and achieving a healthy lifestyle will not happen if you ignore your body's pleas for help. These cues are there for a reason. They aren't meant to be medicated, put off, or ignored. Taking care of yourself means paying attention. It means being intentional about your health and wellbeing by investing in it as you would anything else of great importance.

THE MINDSET OF INTENTION: HEALTHY INVESTMENTS

Kevin Klimowski and Jodi Nicholson, authors of *Million-aire Secrets in You,* discovered that they could give the same set of instructions to five different financial advisors with completely different results. Some of them would do really well, while others would fail completely. This was so frustrating they wondered— what was the key that made such a difference as to whether or not they succeeded?

What they discovered was that success is 80 percent mindset and only 20 percent skill. If the financial planner believed he could do it, he did. *Deciding* that you are going to get something done is more than half the battle. Productive habits can be developed even if the skill isn't yet there, and good habits eventually lead to success. In other words, it's what you think that counts.

WHY ARE YOU SO HAPPY?

Nishangan Thiyagarajah is a teacher at a technical institute in Sri Lanka. One day while doing a school project, he had the opportunity to meet Sussil, our mission-driven advisor from Chapter Five. After talking with Sussil for just 15 minutes, something was rekindled in Nishangan. He set up a date and time to work with Sussil, and from that point onward things shifted in Nishangan. His friends noticed it. His students noticed it. Everyone who sees Nishangan notices it and they ask him, "Why are you so happy?"

It wasn't that Nishangan had suddenly struck gold. He still had his same job, same apartment, same problems. His looks hadn't changed, except that he smiled more. The difference was on the inside. After his meeting, Nishangan could feel change happening inside him and as a result, he didn't just look happy, he *was* happy. Nishangan writes in his own words:

I understand now that my strength is my determination of Self. I always have the ability to think positively, and thinking positively makes me happy. This is my responsibility. Now, I can align my thoughts with my goals and because of that, I am the richest man in the world.

We talked earlier in Chapter Two about the human assets of time, energy, and the ability of our thoughts to have an impact on our physical circumstances. Living healthier begins with thinking healthier. *Cleaning up your act starts with the running track inside your mind.* What are your thoughts about your body, your health, and your ability to exercise? Are these thoughts true? Do those thoughts make you feel lousy or good? Are there other thoughts that you could choose, thoughts that you believe to be true but that might be more helpful?

For example, let's say you are thinking, "I'm too tired to go outside and play catch with my nephew." That might be true, but is there another thought, a more helpful thought, equally true? How about: "If I go outside and play catch for five minutes, I will feel better." If both thoughts are true, why not chose the one that makes you feel better, feel happier, and leads to more positive physical action? As our friend Nishangan realized, it is our responsibility to choose healthier thoughts. No one can get inside our heads and do that for us.

HOW TO MAKE POSITIVE INVESTMENTS

We've all been told that exercise is good for you. But what do you think about it? Don't have the time? Never been good at running? Can't hold a yoga posture to save your life?

It doesn't matter how skilled you are in your chosen area of physical activity. What matters is your intention to do it. Make a commitment to exercise and your success is 80 percent underway. Make the decision to choose helpful thoughts and you will already start feeling better. Apply the same kind of drive that propels you to meet those deadlines and turn it into a new, healthy investment. An investment in exercise will produce dividends every single day. Physical activity doesn't just show up in most people's daily routines unless it is planned for. Exercise must be done with the same kind of intention as growing a business or earning a promotion. You draw up a plan and then commit to it. You show up when you are scheduled, and you do what you said you would do.

If you're intention is to exercise five days a week, schedule it in. *From 12 to 1, Wednesday through Sunday, that is when I go to the gym.* When 12 o'clock on a Wednesday comes rolling around and you are sitting at your desk, you will get up and go change into your gym clothes. It's that simple. There might be a deadline, a last-minute meeting that cropped up, or a problem with daycare. There might be several factors occurring at once, all conspiring to get you to stay and keep working. But this is an appointment. This is a scheduled event as necessary as the staff meeting. Chances are, you don't really want to go to the staff meeting, either, but it's mandatory. So you go. Just go and put your half hour or forty minutes in at the gym and be done with it.

Think of it as an automatic deposit into your health savings account. Do it at the times you have set and it will become just as automatic and, eventually, just as painless. (There will still be plenty of days when you don't want to go, but on those days, go anyway.) If negative thoughts crop up such as, *I look stupid on the treadmill,* or, *I don't have any time for myself,* take responsibility for those thoughts. Find a new thought that you believe could be true, one that makes you feel better, and intentionally think that thought instead. For example, *I look like a determined person on the treadmill.* Or, *I am going to fit into my skinny jeans by my birthday.* This method is what I call "Find and Replace" and it can be a helpful mindset for making healthy investments in multiple areas in our life, including the conundrum of what to eat.

FIND AND REPLACE

Many people start the New Year with the intention of eating better, but then end up repeating the same old habits pretty early on. With regard to eating healthy, the same kind of intention is required. You must make it a priority, and if you are confused about what a healthy choice is, raise your IQ about the subject. Food is a large topic. Thousands of books have been written about this one area alone, mainly because most people *are* confused. Is fat good or bad? What constitutes whole grain, and can high fructose corn syrup really kill you? If you have questions, find the answers by asking your doctor or a nutritionist, or seeking the advice of those around you who have a healthy lifestyle. What you will find, if you haven't figured it out already, is that for the most part eating right is mainly common sense.

Most of us know what is good and bad for us. We may not admit it, but deep down we know a bag of potato chips isn't really in the vegetable food group. Maybe junk food isn't your particular problem, but if you've been wondering how to change poor eating habits into healthy investments, I can offer a strategy that has worked for me.

The purpose of food is to provide fuel. A food closest to its natural form provides the most energy. (An apple, for example, or an egg.) What eating better really comes down to then is making better choices. I prefer to think of this as utilizing the "find and replace" method because, as we learned earlier, mindset is more than half the battle.

A little baby picks up a stick covered with dirt and puts it in her little mouth. The mother, without missing a beat, calmly hands the baby a teething ring and slides the stick out of her mouth with the other hand. This method is recommended by pediatricians and parenting experts everywhere and is known as "find and replace." If the mother were to just walk up to the child and grab the stick out of her hands, a battle would ensue. The child would cry and pitch a fit. There is a little child in all of us who does the same thing every time we hear the word *no*. This is especially true with regard to our treats.

The key to success when investing in healthy eating is to find better choices and replace them with those that are not. Focus on what you *can* have. You can find plenty of literature about what those good choices might look like. Just remember, you are more likely to succeed if you go about it with a helpful mindset. Instead of taking food away, you are giving yourself good and nurturing meals. Think of it this way and then act on it. Replace the thought, *I can't have that packaged brownie*, with the thought, *I am going to make a hot nourishing meal for myself at home*. A blueprint for sound nutrition will provide you with the long-term benefits of both a strong mind and body.

HOW TO DEAL WITH STRESS

Making better choices with regard to the food we eat and setting aside time to exercise are two very positive steps toward reducing stress. The American Heritage Dictionary defines *stress* as "a mentally or emotionally upsetting condition occurring in response to adverse external influences and capable of affecting physical health." Go ahead and say that three times fast. But it's interesting to note that this definition of stress in relation to our health is not present in the dictionaries printed seventy years ago. Doctors have reached a new understanding of stress and the scope of its adverse health effects. Its ability to weaken the immune system has now been proven. The link between stress and ulcers is so profound, even medication can't put a permanent stop to the damage. Doctors have also made stunning discoveries about the profound connection between mind and body.

The term *stress* comes from the use as applied to physics—the internal resistance of a body to applied force or a system of forces. The key word here is *resistance*.

We experience stress when we *resist* or internally reject what is occurring. If we're late for work and the traffic light turns red *again* before we've moved one single inch, our muscles tighten and we might hit the steering wheel. Our body is responding to our mind's rejection of the red light. We don't want it to be red, we resent having to stop, and as a result, we experience stress or the applied force of resistance. Even small stresses like these add up. Increased heart rate, a rise in blood pressure, muscular tension, irritability, and depression are all physical characterizations of stress.

When an elk is in the wild, peacefully eating grass, it experiences normal body functions. The heart beats slowly, the stomach digests the food, and everything flows along. When a cougar shoots out the tall grass, the elk goes into flight mode. As he runs for his life, his body experiences stress and several things happen. His stomach shuts down, no longer digesting food. If the elk is a female, even her cycle of ovulation is interrupted. All the normal functions of the body are altered, focusing energy on one thing only—survival.

Now this makes sense for an elk in the wild. But why would you want to do this to your own body just because of a light change? Yet that is what happens when we are under stress.

Our bodies react to what the mind tells it, regardless of whether the danger is real or imagined.

This means that if the idea of being late for work causes you stress, then that is how your body will respond. There are many people who live in a state of heightened stress like this for the majority of their days. Research now shows that our bodies react to this constant state of stress by storing or holding fat. This is your body's way of protecting you against the "danger" it keeps being told that you are in. Make a decision to reduce the stress levels in your life and the rewards to your health will be far reaching.

CREATE FAVORABLE CONDITIONS

As with eating right and exercise, managing stress begins with a new mindset. We are accustomed to thinking that if we resist something it will go away. We are under the delusion that we can control it somehow. To resist the fact of a red light is the mental equivalent of a temper tantrum. Any time you experience stress, it is because you are resisting what is occurring. The natural way to end the stress, then, would be to accept what is occurring. Of course, this is much easier said than done.

Coach Steve D'Annunzio writes that of all the disciplines he has taught his students over the years, non-attachment is both the most misunderstood and the most beneficial. He writes:

> Non-attachment is the ultimate form of caring, in which you consciously free yourself from outside forces beyond your control that are weakening and draining.

We cannot control when the lights turn red. We cannot control whether or not the person on the other end of the phone will say yes or no, or what time the meeting will end. The same is true of the goals we set for ourselves—we know the steps we must take to achieve them, but sometimes, things happen that are out of our control. We plan to finish shooting the film by Thursday, but an ice storm hits the city. We have a goal to put in one day of overtime a week, but daycare calls and Sally has a fever.

The list can go on and on. Instead of focusing on goals and becoming attached to certain outcomes, to things "going your way," Steve teaches his students to focus instead on creating favorable conditions for the desired outcome. This shift will allow you to focus on what you *can* do.

By taking charge of the things that are in your control, you can then release yourself from the responsibility of those things that aren't.

You made sure to be in your car, dressed, and ready for work by 7:00 A.M. sharp. There was a terrible accident on I-94, and now traffic is backed up. You created conditions favorable to getting to work on time, but something happened outside your control. No need to hit the steering wheel. No need to stop your bodily functions. Calmly give your boss a call and tell him of the delay. You might be surprised at what happens. Because you remained calm and didn't pollute your body with negative mental energy, you left the door open for other opportunities to come your way. Who knows what will happen next?

Creating favorable conditions allows us to remain flexible and to go with the flow of life. With regard to that scheduled time for exercise, if something happens outside of your control—the gym is closed due to a small fire, an emergency at home, an illness—you can roll with the punches and trust that you will be there tomorrow or make up for the lost time. You can release any thoughts you might have of being a failure or not getting it done.

As best as you can in all possible situations, focus on creating favorable conditions. Be clear about what you can control and what you cannot, then take the steps that can be taken. This will replace language such as *I need* and *I want* with the proactive tools of preference, choice, and creative action.

ARREST YOUR STRESS

Leo Babauta, author of the *Time* magazine top 25 blog Zen Habits, shared his method for assessing his stress level in a 2014 post titled, "Overwhelmed and Stressed? Do a Stress Assess." Because Leo made the intentional choice not to copyright his material, I am able to share our version of his test with you here. If you find this process helpful and want to learn more about his philosophy on healthy eating and exercise, visit Leo's page at ZenHabits.net.

Some days are harder than others when it comes to stress. If you've got a lot going on or are having trouble sleeping, you can arrest your stress by taking yourself through the following three simple steps:

Step #1: Make a list of everything that's on your mind or causing you stress. This list might include work projects, financial tasks, or little requests from others that require your mental space. Don't worry about the order or nature of these stressors, just put them down as they occur to you.

Even if you are unable to go beyond this step, just getting all the swirling thoughts out of your head and onto the paper (or digital tablet) will help you to feel more relaxed. You won't have to worry about remembering everything, for one thing!

Step #2: Make a note next to each item on your list that offers a solution to the stressor. For example, if one item on your list is, "Send Mom a birthday present," you might write down, "Order the RichLife 10 Investments book from Amazon." (Yes, that was shameless promotion. Forgive me.)

There might be some items on your list for which you can't immediately offer a solution. That's okay. These might be large projects such as "get a website" or a personal problem or situation on your mind. Simply acknowledge it for now as a stressor. These larger items might require three or four tasks to accomplish. Or you might scribble next to those items, "think about this while on the treadmill."

Step #3: Prioritize and eliminate. Look at your list and place a letter or number to indicate what items you will tackle first. Also put in a time frame when you will tackle said task. For example, you might have, "Draft proposal," as priority A. Next to that you would assign the time 9 to 11 a.m. Once you have identified your priorities—those things which must get done today—and mapped out a time chart, it will become clear which items on your list can be eliminated, cancelled, or postponed for another time.

Be realistic about what you can get done today. Can you ask someone to cancel? Could you get out of a commitment? How about just letting something go? The best way to manage stress is to make arrangements now to prevent stress later. For example, you might move dinner back an hour and let everybody know now, rather than having to disappoint them later. Simple adjustments like this can give you a surprising amount of physical relief, helping your muscles to relax so you don't have to rush around and worry about running out of time.

Doing this little exercise takes anywhere from 10 to 20 minutes of your time, but it can go a long way toward increasing efficiency and reducing stress. To quote Leo directly, "You'll be relieving yourself of burdens, and finding focus. That's worth 20 minutes of your life."

REFLECT AND RECHARGE

In his *New York Times* bestselling book, *The Power of Now*, Eckhart Tolle writes: "Growth is usually considered positive, but nothing can grow forever. If growth, of whatever kind, were to go on and on, it would eventually become monstrous and destructive. The down cycle is absolutely essential...."

You can learn this from Mother Nature—cycles are her secret to growth and rebirth. What are the trees doing during winter, when they are not growing leaves? What about the tulip and daffodil bulbs? Or the acorn before it becomes a tree? Most of us have a hard time justifying "doing nothing." Down times are needed by all living things, but do we allow them for ourselves? Plan for them? Schedule them in?

Remember our security system analogy at the beginning of the chapter? Sometimes the alarm goes off, and all that is needed is a reset. The same is true for our bodies. No major repairs, nothing is broken, and there are no "intruders." But it is time to reset your system. It's time to reflect and recharge.

EARTH CYCLES

Elite athletes perform with intense vigor and stamina at the point when they are under the most pressure to do so. Amidst screaming fans, with cameras and lights all over the place, the athlete stays focused, whether at a professional football game or an Olympic event. How do they consistently do this? How do they create the conditions favorable to playing at the top of their game? Their secret is programmed right into their profession.

They achieve peak performance during game times by employing the secret of downtime.

Athletes perform in cycles. Sports have a season or a time of year for which they were designed. Football is not played seven days a week, fifty-two weeks a year. In fact, *none of these sports are.* During the non-game weeks, athletes practice, work on physical conditioning, or *rest.* They have periods of time built into their schedule when recharging mentally, emotionally, and physically is the sole task. Being at the "top of your game" or even just "in game form" requires intense focus and concentration. We are not capable of sustaining that type of concentration every day, all day, year after year. Nor would you want to. Athletes need the time off-camera, out of view of spectators. So do the tulip bulbs and the seedlings. So does everybody.

Our forbearers lived by the earth's cycles, especially those who were involved in an agrarian lifestyle. Because they were unable to farm during winter, those months became their time for rest and planning. The hardest, most focused work came during the times of planting and harvest, just before and after the time of rest. The sun was the clock that kept their schedule. They got up with the sunrise and went to bed at sunset. In the fall when the daylight was long, they would use every last drop of light to bring in their crop, and when the sun went down they sometimes relied on the "harvest moon." Cycles dictated and directed their entire lives, allowing for a natural order of give and take. It would be pointless for them to run out to their fields at midnight to try and hurry their crop along. Even more foolish to dig up the plant to see what the roots were doing, as if that could help.

MONTHS AND MINUTES

There is a scene near the end of Larry McMurtry's book, *Boone's Lick*, which comes to mind here. The Cecil family of seven, including a baby still nursing, travels by covered wagon through the Wild West. They journey from Boone's Lick, Missouri to Fort Phil Kearny, Wyoming, leaving late enough in the fall to encounter cold nights, flooded rivers and streams, wagon breakdowns, and a constant harassment of Indians.

Near the book's end, the family finally approaches Fort Phil Kearny. By now that little baby is toddling around, and 15-year-old Shay Cecil has shot and killed his first bear. No one in the family is quite sure why they had to leave their home to spend months out on the road, but their mother, Mary Margret, said it was something she had to do, and once this mother decided on a thing, it was a thing that got done.

It was Mary Margret who drove the wagon into Fort Phil Kearny that day. It was Shay who first recognized his dad, joshing with a couple of woodcutters sitting with their backs against some old wagon wheels. Dick Cecil saw their wagon coming, but could hardly believe his eyes. His wife, Mary Margret, stops the mules and hands the reins over to her brother-in-law, Seth, who offers to go with her, but she declines the help. With the entire family watching, Mary walks over to her husband of fifteen years, the man who is father to all five of her children, including four who had died and the baby in the wagon whom Dick hadn't even seen yet. She has a conversation with this man, says what she came to say. Then Mary comes back to the wagon, climbs up, and takes the reins.

Her brother-in-law stares at her in astonishment.

"That's it? A two-minute conversation? After months of crossing the prairie through Indians and bad weather, we come all this way out here for a *two-minute conversation*?"

And Mary Margret says to him, "Some things take months, other things take just minutes."

PACING YOURSELF

In today's society, people drive themselves relentlessly to work, work, work, and seldom if ever take the needed time to rest. Rest has somehow become equated with laziness and non-productivity. Because they cannot abide this in others, they don't allow it in themselves. The individual with an aggressive, driven personality who is striving to become successful finds it nearly impossible to *allow* himself to slow down, let alone to stop, take a break, and rest.

When Mary Margret drove that wagon across the prairie, there were countless hours of monotony and rest. Sometimes there were entire days when they couldn't move forward at all. But she had created for herself favorable conditions that would eventually get her to the fort. Her pace would have sent most A-type personalities running for the hills, but Mary Margret knew that some things just take longer than other things. She used her time wisely, the way athletes do when they rest, train, and condition before a game.

Mary Margret was mentally prepared for her "game" so that when the time came for her big showdown, it took minutes to get the job done. And it was done well. Her husband was left speechless.

Some things take minutes, other things take months.

If you can remember this, you can stay within the flow of life. You will use the momentum created in up cycles for increased productivity; when there are down times or slower cycles, you will use that time effectively to recharge and *reflect*. To gather your thoughts, plan, daydream, or maybe (gasp!) even take a nap.

THE IMPORTANCE OF TRUE REST

In today's society, we don't travel by covered wagon and we don't work by the sun. We have light available to us twenty-four hours a day, and because of this resting gets pushed aside. We think if we can work longer and harder, we will get ahead of the next guy. This might be helpful to apply to certain projects, but as a mindset and a way of life, it is both unhealthy and unsustainable, and, as you will see in the following example, unnecessary.

The average fast food franchise hopes to achieve $800,000 a year in gross revenue. The gold standard of the industry is the golden arches, with their revenues reaching $1.2 to $1.3 million a year *per franchise*. These are impressive numbers. Yet there is one competitor relatively young by comparison that is turning these numbers on their side.

When Truett Cathy started the Chick-Fil-A franchise, he set aside Sunday as a day of rest, both for himself and all employees. He did this in keeping with his personal set of beliefs. Not everyone who works for Chick-Fil-A is a Christian, but they all sure benefit from the rest. These restaurants routinely average *$3 million per franchise* in gross revenue. And remember, they are open *one day less* per week.

These numbers attest to the fact that investing in rest, slowing down, and stopping does in the end pay off. All this rush, hurry, and pressure adds stress and drains us of energy. Like all living things, human beings operate in cycles. It's time to retrain ourselves to recognize the ebb and flow of energy cycles in our own life. It's time to honor them, give them the time they need, and give ourselves *rest*.

For most people, this will be a learning process requiring a paradigm shift. It doesn't seem to make sense that a restaurant open one day less per week would generate nearly *double* the revenue as compared to the competitor who is open all the time. Yet it *does* make sense that a person who has had a day off will come back to work refreshed.

You don't have to take my word for it—give it a try yourself. Start listening to the cycles occurring in your own life and instead of resisting them—which will create stress—go with them. Use your down time efficiently as you would any other opportunity and schedule in time to rest and recharge.

GAME WEEKS AND BUFFER DAYS

In my professional life, I have created a cycle using the ebb and flow of my own energy levels that has really come to work for me. The more difficult and challenging projects are set aside for three weeks out of the month. I call these my "Game Weeks," which will make sense for you sports fans; you can, of course, call them anything you want. During these weeks, I make a conscious effort to move projects forward. I am aggressive about setting meetings and agendas, working to create favorable conditions.

On the fourth week of every month, I shift gears. I set aside this week for working on more restful and creative projects. These might be things I am doing for my own personal gratification, projects that won't earn immediate profit, or they are simply enjoyable activities such as reading and outings or meeting with friends or clients. I call these weeks my "Bye Weeks."

I've found that for me, personally, this cycle works great. When I come back from that "rest" week, I am more invigorated and recharged to return to the other, more challenging tasks at hand. But a cycle of weeks may not work for you. There are other models you can try.

Some teachings suggest creating a system of "days" rather than weeks. Out of a seven-day week, you set aside four of them for the harder, more intense work. This is when you take care of those things which are especially challenging, important, or tedious. Two days are set aside for preparation, ideally occurring before the intense work days, when you would study, research, and plan. Dan Sullivan, author of *Strategic Coach,* refers to these as "Buffer Days." Add into this mix one free day where no work at all is done for a 24-hour period, and you have your cycle. This rest day presents the perfect opportunity to relax, reflect, and recharge.

POWER HOUR

While this system of days works for many people, my plan of alternating weeks works better for me. However, it took me a while to learn that. There is no right or wrong way here, only what works best for you personally. It might take a number of experiments to see what is the most advantageous for you and your needs. A good place to start is by noticing what your natural tendencies are. If you droop around three o'clock in the afternoon, plan for that. Maybe for you, your cycle is one of hours. If early morning is when you find yourself to be the most creative, slot in those tasks requiring optimum brain power.

Most people will find that their bodies go through a kind of "mini" cycle almost every day. Stopping to recharge on a daily basis is a great idea and can be done by scheduling in time for prayer or meditation. A time for quieting your mind and getting your emotions settled. Some people prefer this to be at the beginning of their day or during their "lunch" hour, while others feel it's more beneficial at the end of the day just before going to bed.

Personally, I practice what I have come to call my *RichLife Power Hour* in the morning. The inspiration for this came from one of my mentors, Jack Canfield, who got the idea from Canadian speaker Azim Jamal. For my RichLife version, I set aside one hour during my work week, and I divide it thus:

- 20 minutes of physical exercise (body)

- 20 minutes of gratitude/prayer (soul)

- 20 minutes of reading something positive, uplifting, or educational (mind)

This can be rotated and adjusted to fit your needs, but should include the three areas of mind/body/soul. Make this a habitual part of your everyday life. Treat the time spent in these areas as automatic deposits into your health account, and you will see the many benefits of this practice begin to add up. I find that some of my best ideas come to me during my quiet time first thing in the morning. The solution to a problem will just pop into my head, or an idea I have been turning over will suddenly make sense to me from a new angle. I could have spent months at my desk, trying to come up with an idea that took only two minutes of quiet to arrive.

Like Mary Margret said, some things take months, other things take minutes. Give yourself a period of quiet every day, and discover how this secret can also work for you.

BENEFICIAL GETAWAYS

In addition to daily recharge, there should also be a time, at least quarterly, when you can get away and totally shut down. This doesn't mean going to a crowded vacation spot and filling your days with travel and sightseeing. Many people going on so called "vacations" come back looking more frazzled than when they left. What I am referring to here is a time when you can come to a total stop.

It's amazing what can happen on a creative level when there is an atmosphere of peace and quiet. Not only have I experienced this for myself, but I have witnessed incredible transformation in the lives of others.

> Those who feel they must continually go, go, go, without ever giving themselves a moment of rest, suddenly realize that by stopping they actually become more productive.

The place where I like to go is a cabin in the woods, and I go there alone to write, plan, create, and think. For me, it is necessary to get away from life's daily commitments and all the distractions. The money I spend on this trip is not an expense, it's an investment. I will admit, however, that when I first started taking these little getaways, they did seem more like a luxury. I wasn't accustomed to giving myself time to do "nothing." That way of thinking has long since changed. I now view this time as a necessity. It may look to others like I am doing "nothing," but when I come back home, I am twice as productive. That's why I consider it one of my prime investments.

I never wait to see "if I have the time," and I encourage you not to wait, either. Again, there is no right or wrong here—only what fits into your life and is right for you. The important thing is not the when or how, but committing to these beneficial getaways on a regular basis.

Whether it's daily, monthly, or quarterly, determine that you will *make* the time, as I did, to stop and get rejuvenated. This is all a part of returning to the natural cycles of life that have been lost in our noisy, sometimes crazy, nonstop lifestyles. I guarantee your body will be glad for the break.

PORTFOLIO BUILDER

Investing in your own good health is one of the least risky investments there is. Those who believe they can keep up an endless, nonstop schedule of all work and no rest or play are in for a rude awakening. Sooner or later, the body rebels. It might be heart problems, high blood pressure, or ulcers. It might be a weakened immune system or a dozen other problems that have been linked to stress. Whatever it is, the result will be a *forced* time of rest, meaning it will happen regardless of whatever else is going on in your life. Why not be proactive?

Making investments in your health can be an enjoyable process. Eat well, schedule in regular rest and exercise, and make time for yourself to totally get away. Taking care of your health in this way not only increases your productivity, it lowers your stress levels and leads to a better overall quality of life. Relationships will improve and time with family will become more enjoyable. Make taking care of your primary asset a priority every day. This is your RichLife we are creating. Let's make sure that you are around to enjoy it.

THE TAKE-AWAYS

- Without your health, enjoyment of all you have accomplished and gained decreases or is lost.

- We experience stress when we resist or internally reject what is occurring.

- Our bodies react to what our minds tell them, regardless of whether the danger is real or imagined.

- As best as you can in all possible situations, focus on creating favorable conditions.

- The secret to achieving peak performance during "game time" is allowing and scheduling down time.

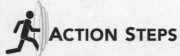

ACTION STEPS

- Which of these three areas of your physical health can you begin investing in today? Exercise? Diet? Rest? Choose the area in which you are weakest and commit to one goal. Be sure to give yourself *what* and *when*. For example, *I will start making my own lunch instead of having a cheeseburger, beginning this Monday.*

- Identify an area of your life that is causing you stress. Divide a piece of paper into two columns and write at the top of one side "I can control" and on the other side "I cannot control." Once you are clear about the controllables, start another list: What can you do to create favorable conditions so you get the result you prefer? Make a list of what you can do, and then set about doing those things.

- Start noticing the thoughts that run through your head on a daily basis. See if you can give yourself a break from those thoughts. While waiting in line or sitting at a red light, tell yourself, "I am just going to take a break from my thoughts for thirty seconds." After your thought break is over, see if you can choose a thought that makes you feel happy.

- Learn to identify events that are not in your control, and see what it feels like if you don't resist them. Start with the small things first like the barking dog or the red light. Work your way up to the bigger things like missing a meeting or deadline.

- Do some thinking about the ebb and flow of your own daily schedule. Take a look at the calendar and come up with a plan that allows for "game time" and "bye time." Give it a trial run of one month and see how it feels.

- Begin to make plans for your own quiet getaway— one with no work involved.

- **Bonus Gift**: Download your free copy of the Action Guide for *The RichLife: Ten Investments for True Wealth* at www.RichLifeActionGuide.com.

Investment #10

CONTRIBUTION

"The generous man will be prosperous, and
he who waters will himself be watered."
–Proverbs 11:25, NASB

SETTING ASIDE SEED

In the last chapter, I referred to our forbearers and how they lived by the cycles of the seasons. There were seasons of planting, seasons of harvest, and seasons of rest. There is yet another aspect of this life that was vital to their wellbeing—the setting aside of seed.

A part of every harvest—be it potatoes, corn, or wheat—was set aside as "seed grain" for planting the following year. The seed potatoes would not be eaten, neither would the seed corn or wheat. It would be a foolish farmer indeed who ate his seed. Without that, there would be no future crop.

Sowing and reaping is a cycle we can all understand, even in this day and age where fewer and fewer of us are farmers. What you put into the ground and tend to is what will grow. What is neglected will in turn wither and perish. By the same token, care must be taken with regard to how we treat our harvest.

> A portion of every crop must be set aside and not consumed.

Using this as an analogy for our RichLife, it is essential that a portion of all we receive, be it money, goods, or service, be designated as the "seed" for our future tomorrows. This is what we put back out into our community, in the form of individual gifts or acts of service to others. The practice of giving insures the continual flow of riches into our own future lives.

HABIT FIRST, MONEY SECOND

One of the biggest mistakes people make is thinking they have to wait until they are a big success before they can afford to be generous. This kind of thinking will often ensure that neither happens, meaning *you will neither become generous* nor *successful*. Giving and receiving are connected, mutually dependent on one another just like the seed and the crop. It is one of those natural laws that function regardless of whether or not you are aware of it. The sayings are many: *You only get what you give, What goes around comes around, You reap what you sow* and so on and so forth. You have all heard this said before; you may even already subscribe to the idea. But with regard to giving back, *what are your habits?*

Imagine you have $100 in the bank and someone calls and asks you for a donation. It is an organization you value and would like to support, but you tell them, "I'm sorry, I can't do it this month. Call me in a year." You are waiting to have $1,000 in the bank, because then you will feel more comfortable with giving. A year later the organization calls you back, and you have $1,000 in the bank, and $1,000 worth of bills to go along with it. You tell them the same thing. "I'm sorry, I can't do it. I don't have enough money." When will you have enough? When will you feel comfortable? *Never*. Waiting to be generous keeps you trapped in *scarcity mentality*. These are the thoughts of *not enough* we have talked about earlier. Thinking this way will keep you tight and afraid, holding on to what you have. The irony here is that this tightness and holding—which is done as a means of protection—only serves to keep you closed off from receiving good, including money, success, and any other help that might come your way.

Dr. Wayne Dyer is known for saying, "Generosity is a function of the heart, not of the wallet." In other words, it's not about the monetary amount, it's about the habit. Giving can be done in a multitude of ways, large and small. It can be done with a smile as well as with coins. If you are not in the habit of giving to others, you won't do it regardless of the amount that sits in your bank accounts. Giving is something you must begin doing now on a daily basis, in your community, among individuals, and even to yourself. Any gift counts—gifts of time, talent, money, and stewardship, even the gift of a smile. And in turn, there are endless ways to receive.

Whatever you put out into the world will in turn come back to you. With regard to creating your RichLife, giving back is a habit that must be put in place in order to achieve the balance of true abundance. Giving back is akin to scattering seeds far and wide. This means that, regardless of the climate in your particular area, someone somewhere will reap a positive harvest, and a portion of that will in turn find its way back to you.

GIVING TO THE COMMUNITY

I recognize that I've had many opportunities in my life due to the help and generosity of those around me. Many people helped shape who I am today, and many people helped me to get where I am. As a boy growing up, there were many times an adult gave me a hand up with something just because they knew my father. They were "paying it forward" or returning a kindness that was shown to them. Now, as an adult myself, I want to keep "paying it forward." I want to be a good steward to the generosity that was shown me by giving a hand up to others whenever I can.

The Jimmy Henderson Adult Literacy Scholarship was originally founded in honor of my father by my mom, my sister, and me. Over the years the amount of the scholarship has grown, and in the last couple of years it has become part of the projects supported by RichLife Advisors. Because of the seed planted by my father all those years ago, this effort continues to grow on into the future, and I can't tell you how happy this makes me.

The goal of this scholarship is to provide monetary support for adults seeking to further their education. These are individuals in the community who never graduated from high school or, in some cases, never even attended. As an adult in their forties, fifties, and even sixties, they come around to realizing their life purpose and require further education. They need to go to college. And before they can even get there, they must complete their GED. This is where the scholarship program comes in.

What I love about this program is watching how someone's life can completely turn around in five years. It would be easy for these adults to look at their situation and say, "It's hopeless. It will take too long. I can't even read." It would be easy to blame circumstances, family, and a lousy economy. Many people do choose that route. But what I find inspiring is what happens when people decide to take responsibility and change their own situation. I want to be a part of that. These are the people who need our support, be it in the form of encouragement, money, or resources. As they are able to go forward with their lives, they in turn give back to the community by developing and sharing their giftings and talents.

The good compounds in the best interests of everyone. Talk about a good investment.

But it gets even better. A funny thing happens when you support the success of others. *You, in turn, become even more of a success.* I can't tell you the number of new clients I have gotten just from doing one act of community service. People resonate with this idea. Those who have experienced it in their lives, as I have, want to keep it going, and they will seek to do business with those who operate in this way. But the real key here, the secret to giving, is that it must be done in the spirit of pure service. *You must give with no expectation of anything in return.* At times this is easy. Other times, it may be more challenging, but rewards often come from unexpected directions.

I WOULD LIKE FOR YOU TO DO SOMETHING

In January of 2004, a young mother by the name of Vicki Moore came across a story on the Internet about the everyday reality faced by millions of girls and women living in India. The story she read told of the more than two hundred women forced into prostitution daily. How they are sold or kidnapped into the sex trade as early as age five. How these women are held captive, beaten, raped, and humiliated. How they are made to believe that their only real value is the price that their body will bring. By their late teens, the majority of these girls are considered "used up" and are cast out onto the streets to survive on their own. With little to no skill sets and not enough money to maintain themselves, these girls return to prostitution as a means of survival, and the hopeless cycle continues.

According to the Human Rights Watch, there are approximately fifteen million prostitutes in India today, and at least half of them may be infected with the Human Immunodeficiency Virus (HIV). These are women and girls, mothers and daughters, most of them between the ages of fifteen and thirty-five. Back in 2004, Vicki Moore was a stay-at-home mom with children of her own.

She had no experience with human trafficking but found the global statistics alarming. The disturbing stories broke her heart, and she could not get them out of her mind. That day in the comfort of her own home, Vicki Moore asked the question, "Why isn't anyone doing anything about this?"

And then she heard the answer, *I would like for you to do something.*

RAHAB'S ROPE: HEALING ONE BY ONE

Prior to 2004, Moore had visited India several times, working with missionary friends in an orphanage and at a Bible college. But she had never before been exposed to the realities of the sex trade. As it happened, Moore had an upcoming trip planned for May of that year, and so instead of waiting for someone else to do something about the fate of these women and girls, Ms. Moore followed her heart. Instead of thinking the problem too big or herself too small, Ms. Moore took action. She planned, held meetings, and gave a new directive for her trip to the city of Bangalore, opening the eyes of her missionary friends to the crisis. Writes one volunteer:

> Everywhere we looked we saw hundreds of young women sitting or standing around. As we walked by, many of them stopped us (and asked us) to pray for them. The pastor who was with us had told us there were between 15,000 to 20,000 women working in that area daily but we had been skeptical. Until we began to walk around. We could see through the doorways into the hovels. We literally waded through sewage and garbage and shook hands with dirty, half-naked children.

In December of 2004, a short eleven months after stumbling across that first Internet story, Moore held the first Annual Christmas Celebration to introduce Rahab's Rope to a group of women who had been used and abused for most of their lives, with no sign that their reality would ever change.

Moore recalls, "We believe nothing happens in our lives by chance and timing is God appointed. As God was opening my eyes to the women in crisis in India, I was also taking an Old Testament Bible class and studying the story of Rahab, the prostitute found in the book of Joshua. The rope in the story represents Rahab's rescue both physically and spiritually, and there is a high probability that Rahab made the rope herself. Our hope is that, just as the rope that Rahab made represents her rescue, the skills taught to the women at our women's centers will represent their physical and spiritual rescue as well. It seemed fitting for Rahab's Rope to be our name."

In keeping with their mission, Rahab's Rope has spent the last decade teaching women skills and giving them hope and opportunity where none had been before. From a small, rented flat in Bangalore, they worked to provide training and a safe, loving environment; in Goa they founded a medical clinic; and in Mumbai they worked directly in the brothels. They have provided health and nutrition, groceries, hygiene education, and supplies; they have provided vocational training as well as basic education. They have also provided medical needs, including a life-saving surgery for one girl whose sinus cavities had been horribly destroyed through multiple beatings.

More recently, the organization has expanded its efforts at home, opening a new store and warehouse space from their operations base in Gainesville, Georgia. From here they receive and sell goods such as jewelry and patchwork handbags made by the young women in Rahab's Rope centers in India, as well as from artisans in other countries. The profits from the store fund the production center in India, two after-care homes, and the education and training programs that have expanded to include four stations in India. As more girls enter the program daily, trained volunteers travel to the prevention projects in Goa and the aftercare programs in Bangalore to provide comfort, tutoring, and life skills training.

One volunteer writes: "Twenty-three women are connected by more than the arms resting against a neighbor's knee or our common sense of how warm it is growing; we are united in our vulnerability, in our growing realization that to be a woman—especially here in a lower-income area of India—is to be at risk for sex trafficking. Didi asks the girls what they have learned today. A beautiful young woman in a crimson salwar says softly, 'I should tell all of my friends about this. If we tell them one by one, we can stop this.'"

Plans for the organization include reaching out to more girls in additional areas, adding a new safe house for underage girls, and their current work of acquiring and outfitting new housing facilities for women in aftercare. If you would like to find out what you can do to support the ongoing mission of Rahab's Rope, visit their website at www.rahabsrope.com. They offer travel, employment and volunteer opportunities, and the reminder, "What you wish you could do for everyone, do for one."

DO UNTO OTHERS

I have a friend who is in the habit of keeping a five-dollar bill in his pocket. He lives in New York City and every time he goes out, he passes by someone in need. He enjoys dropping his five-dollar bill into their cup or in their hat. Sometimes they are musicians who share their beautiful music, and often he catches a surprised glimpse of gratitude on their face. But there are also the days when he is reprimanded by the friend or colleague walking along with him.

"Why did you just do that?" they ask. "He's just going to use it to buy more booze or drugs."

And my friend replies, "What they do with it is not my concern. The only thing that matters is my reason for giving it."

This goes to the very heart of the word *compassion*. Many people mistake this word to mean pity, or feeling sorry for. The root of the word comes from the Latin *patri* and the Greek *pathein* which means: "to suffer, undergo, or experience." To have compassion for someone literally means to feel their pain as your own. To walk for a minute in their shoes and ask yourself, *How would I like to be treated if I was in that circumstance?*

The Golden Rule sums up the heart of compassion best: "Do unto others as you would have them do unto you."

Author Karen Armstrong defines compassion in *12 Steps to a Compassionate Life* as "an attitude of principled, consistent altruism." Living this way not only adds to your RichLife, but in many ways determines it because the personal benefits of practicing regular altruism improve every area of your life.

In terms of health, Dr. David R. Hawkins describes in *Power Verses Force* how one act of kindness serves to boost the immune system of the giver and the receiver *as well as anyone else who observes* the act of kindness. Doing something as simple as holding the door open for the person behind you physically makes you stronger! So does telling the truth. This is the reason for that "good feeling" we get whenever we are unexpectedly kind or generous to another living thing. It is more than just a feeling. Our bodies are physically strengthened.

Experiencing true compassion for others can also transform a person's life, revealing an unexpected life purpose or mission, as was the case with Vicki Moore, founder of Rahab's Rope. In an interview with Ms. Moore we asked her, "What has the experience of helping these women given back to you?"

Her answer: "A joy and excitement to life that can't be explained. I have met so many wonderful people all across the U.S. and in India who have helped in so many ways, and many have become very good friends. These people have poured into the ministry with their gifts, talents, and finances, and poured into me with their encouragement and kindness. I would never have had this experience had I not been working with these girls in India."

GIVING TO YOURSELF

It is indeed ironic how the selfless act of giving can so truly provide abundance for that very same self. But to reach a place where that kind of giving—and receiving—is possible, one must first remove all inner obstacles. There is a saying that comes to mind here: *Private victories precede public victories*. In other words, the ability to give to others begins with the ability to give to one's self.

Some people have a difficult time treating themselves with the same consideration they give to others. Some people are very hard on themselves. One of the things I talk to my clients about is the one person who never gets paid. Guess who that is? That's right—you. I teach the discipline of *paying yourself first* because, though often neglected, it is the key to a healthy relationship with money.

A lot of people have a hard time saving because everything else seems more important. But if you are *not* paying yourself first, then chances are saving won't happen. Setting aside the "seed," so to speak, must happen before the bills are paid. I recommend having a portion of every paycheck automatically deducted or taken out. Your company's 401(k), 403(b), SEP, or other retirement plan can deduct a percentage of your income pre-tax from your paycheck. You can set up an automatic draft to fund after tax savings like Roth IRAs, brokerage accounts, and savings accounts. You can also set up automatic drafts to fill up separate buckets for emergency savings, car fund, and house maintenance

Some of my most successful clients follow a formula that goes a long way toward developing this discipline, and the formula encompasses giving both to yourself and others. It is a simple breakdown with no gray area. The formula does two things: it teaches you to live below your means, and it makes giving—both to yourself and others—a regular habit. The formula looks something like this:

- An amount you can live off of: 70 percent

- An amount to save: 10 percent

- An amount to go toward debt: 10 percent

- An amount to give away: 10 percent

This breakdown can be adjusted to fit your budget. If you need every penny, it might look like this: 97 percent, 1 percent, 1 percent, 1 percent. The important thing to remember here is you are establishing the discipline of giving, of paying yourself first, and giving back. You are making it a habit, something that happens regularly, something you don't even have to think about. And the really good news is that once the debt is gone and paid off, you can increase what you give—either to yourself or to others—without changing your lifestyle one bit.

Giving to yourself includes the tangible things we talked about in the previous chapter as well as kindness and compassion. Sometimes, we need to take a look at how we treat ourselves before we can improve the way we treat others. This includes the way we invest in and save for our own future. Take the time to find out what private victories are needed in the area of giving in order for growth to happen.

WRAPPED UP IN SELF

On the flip side, there are also people who seem to have blinders on when it comes to the lives of others. These are individuals who are so focused on their individual road to success that they consume and move on. It never occurs to them to contribute or give back, and rarely are they grateful. Whatever they get is never enough, and so they move on to the next thing, consuming even more.

This is a lifestyle that grows ever smaller. This is a person so wrapped up in themselves that they end up missing all of the most valuable things in life. It never occurs to this person to be grateful—or to stop and consider how he or she can make a contribution, let alone to give back on an ongoing basis. This is a person who is eating all of their seed. Consuming takes precedence over everything. Eventually, this will catch up with them.

Do you remember the story I told at the beginning of this book about Richard, the miserable multimillionaire? Where he ended up exemplifies a life of misplaced priorities. His was the road to monetary success that neglected those assets of real value, including his family, health, and wellbeing. Compare that to the life of Vicki Moore, a woman who turned one decision of giving back into a lifetime mission of promoting recovery and opportunity. Ask yourself, who is the richer person?

 ## PORTFOLIO BUILDER

To consume or contribute? This is a key question that all of us must ask ourselves frequently, if not daily.

Contribution is a word not heard much in today's consumer society. It is an old word, like stewardship, that points toward a holistic approach to living in the world. It considers others and encompasses the idea of giving back. This goes hand in hand with the tradition of setting aside the seed for the future crops of tomorrow, to insure that there will be something down the road for us to live on.

Those who ascribe to the holistic idea of a RichLife actively seek ways they can give back to others. They do both—consume and contribute. They are deeply thankful for what they have, which supplies the motivation and the energy for giving back. This giving back can take many different forms:

- The mother who makes room in her busy schedule for one-on-one time with each of her children.

- The businessman who keeps five dollars in his pocket to give away.

- The lady who leaves any coins she drops on the floor knowing it will be a treat for a little kid to find.

- The businessman who washes the dishes for his wife.

- The professional who donates a half hour every week to read to children at an elementary school.

- The volunteer at the church bazaar who sells her baked goods to raise money for a good cause.

- The clerk who tells you to have a nice day after she rings up your groceries.

- The businesswoman who donates regularly to a non-profit charity.

Contributing also refers to the RichLife proponent who is intent on investing in his or her *own* life. This is the person who lives each day intent on adding value to his own life, his family, his community, and the world around him. It is a life that is rich in *giving back*.

Money, health, and aid will always come back to you in your time of need if you practice the wisdom of "setting aside seeds." Giving to the community and to others requires compassion, or the ability to treat others as we would want to be treated. It requires that we consider another's pain or point of view. This may not always be what is convenient. Giving what is needed might ask more of us than we originally prepared for, but having the courage to follow through will lead to greater rewards and a richer tomorrow.

The beautiful thing about giving back is that it has a tendency to multiply in unexpected ways. That's what seeds do—they grow, flower, scatter, and multiply. No one can live a full RichLife without including *contribution* into the equation.

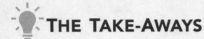 **THE TAKE-AWAYS**

- Like the farmers who reserved a portion of their crop for seeds, we must practice giving as a means to insure the flow of riches into our own future.

- Whatever you put out into the world will in turn come back to you.

- The secret to giving is that it must be done with no expectation of anything in return.

- Make it a practice to live by the Golden Rule: Do unto others as you would have them do unto you.

- Give what is needed, not just what is convenient.

 **ACTION STEPS**

The Giving Experiment

Step One: It has been said that whatever we think the world is not giving us is the very thing we ourselves are not giving to the world. Identify what is missing from your life. This must be a specific answer, not a general one. For example, don't just say "money!" or "financial success." Identify what financial success would look like in your life, for example, "More customers who support and patronize my small business." Instead of saying, "a spouse!" say, "A life partner and friend who accepts me for the way I am and champions my dreams." The answers must be personal. They must resonate and be specific to what you feel is missing from your life.

Step Two: For four weeks make a conscious, intensive effort to give the very thing you feel is missing from your own life. In the two examples mentioned above, some of these actions would be as follows:

- **Example A:** "More customers who support and patronize my small business."

- Stop by other small shops and businesses. Chat with the owners, find out what they do, and if you find it to be valuable, buy something. Buy what your budget allows—no need to go into debt here. A small purchase is just as valuable as a big one.

- Send business to others. When you discover a valuable product, vendor, or shop, send them customers by talking to or emailing your friends, family, and other customers. When you send them gifts from these places, be sure to include a business card or other printed material.

- Be on the lookout for ways that you can support anybody who is an entrepreneur like yourself. These can be unexpected places. For example, buy the pancake mix from the guy in your grocery store who is selling his family's "secret recipe." If you like it and find it to be a quality product, recommend it to neighbors and friends.

- When you see a busy shop or store, instead of grumbling to yourself that they have all the luck, say to yourself, "Good for them!" Champion success whenever you see it. Remember what we discovered in Investment #8 about building your team. The principle of win/win means success for all, not one at the expense of another.

- **Example B:** "A life partner and friend who accepts me for the way I am and champions my dreams."

- Make an effort to overlook the bad habits or idiosyncrasies of others. Notice when resistance to their behavior comes up, and see if you can make room for it. Find out what happens if you decide not to mind the fact that it annoys you.

- Whenever the thought comes up, "Ugh, I hate it when she does that/says that," immediately make a shift. Interrupt the thought and begin searching for something you *do* like. It can be anything, even the color of the shirt they have on. Once you identify it, say it out loud and see where it leads you.

- Ask people not about what work they do, but about what they would like to do. Make it a point to discover the RichLife of one or two people in your life, and then check in with them regularly. It can be a five-minute conversation once a week, or even a text or email. Ask them, *How did the interview go? How's the book coming along? Did you run the 5K?*

Step Three: Evaluate and track. How did it go? Just as important as the concrete things that may have appeared, how did you feel while you were behaving this way? What benefits did you notice to your health, your overall mood? What are the chances you could keep this up for two more weeks and keep building on the momentum you've created?

- **Bonus Step:** Download your free copy of the Action Guide for *The RichLife: Ten Investments for True Wealth* at www.RichLifeActionGuide.com.

THE MASTER INVESTMENT: THE HARD EASY PRINCIPLE

"It's not that I'm so smart. It's just that
I stay with problems longer."
—ALBERT EINSTEIN

We are now nearing the end of the book. We have covered 10 Investments that, if practiced, can lead you down the road to a brilliant RichLife. They might make perfect sense to you, but the question remains, will you make these investments or not? Some of them might sound like a lot of work. Other areas you might feel you already have covered and this is good. But what is it that makes *the ultimate difference* between those who achieve their RichLife and those who do not? The answer is—the Master Investment.

The principle of Hard Easy is what I call the master investment. It is a habit that when applied to any area of your life will make the greatest singular difference. It is also the biggest secret to success that no one is talking about. We are going to talk about it. Application of Hard Easy is your call to action. It is the one thing that you *can* do regardless of age or income that will make the greatest difference between changing your life and not changing your life. Let's take a look at what Hard Easy means and, when applied, what it can do for your RichLife.

LOOKING GOOD

You have just parked your car and are about to get out when you see a sleek black Lamborghini glide into the parking space next to yours. *Man*, you think, *what a sweet ride*. The driver of the car gets out, locks the doors, and bounces up the sidewalk on his way to work. Your eyes follow as he enters one of the tallest, most prestigious office buildings in town. You take a look again at his car and notice he also has a designated parking spot. *Man*, you think to yourself again, *I wish I had it that easy!*

In this chapter we are going to talk about getting to the place of *easy*. In the preceding chapters, we laid out a formula. Now we are going to talk about putting that formula into action.

You've probably noticed the words *Hard Easy* sound like both good news and bad news. Let's start with the hard, because from then on it only gets better. The first thing you need to realize is that the guy you saw parking his Lamborghini *has it easy now* because he was willing *to do the hard first*. You didn't see the ten or fifteen years that came before the moment he pulled that car up next to yours. You didn't see the work it took for him to get there. You only saw that he *arrived*.

The good news is that there is no reason on earth that your time to *arrive* can't happen as well. Steve D'Annunzio refers to Hard Easy as "the life success code breaker." As I mentioned earlier, this is the biggest secret out there to both personal and professional success, yet very few people are doing it. The work required here is both an inner and outer shift, a principle that when applied regularly becomes a habit that can literally transform the rest of your life.

Plato was once quoted as saying, "The beginning is the most important part of the work." We're going to talk about what it takes at the beginning.

DIALING FOR DOLLARS

Most people do "easy hard." They solve their objectives in the easiest manner possible, with the least amount of work. They subscribe to the axiom *work smart not hard*. While there's validity to that saying and a time and place for working smart, the reality is that in most every profession, in order to be successful you've got to work hard up front.

When I first got into the business of financial planning, the percentage of people who didn't make it past their first year was really high. By the second year, the dropout rate was somewhere around 70 percent. As a new financial advisor, it's hard initially to make enough money to pay your bills because it takes a while to develop a residual income. I saw many of my colleagues drop out or fall by the wayside.

But I figured out that if I made cold calls every day with the goal of setting up one appointment a day, I would fill my pipeline. There would always be people for me to meet with, and as long as I was meeting with people, business would happen. I never knew if that business would happen on the first day of the month or the last, and there were cancellations and plenty of times when the appointment or goal didn't happen. But there were also days when I exceeded my goal. I certainly wouldn't call making those cold calls every day *fun*. But I did them. And the hard paid off.

Call reluctance is one of biggest things that keeps people from succeeding, especially at sales or the beginning of a new career. But the key to success is to push past the dread and make the doing a habit.

And I did used to dread making those calls. A lot of it was cold calling; I was lucky if it was lukewarm. A lot of people I knew were calling as many as 100 people a day. But I set a number goal that was possible for me and I stuck with it. Instead of letting the dread immobilize me, I focused on doing the activity and it became a habit.

I learned how doing could become a habit when I interned with a large brokerage house. It was my task to go upstairs to a room with this list of over 1,000 people. And before I left every day, I had to call 100 of them. I really can't say I enjoyed that, but it taught me the discipline. Later on, as a financial planner just starting out, it was making those cold calls every day that made the difference. Those calls, as hard as they were to make, gave me enough people to work with. I never would have gotten to the place where I am today if I hadn't been willing to push past the dread, buckle down, and do the hard first.

HARD EASY HABIT

My friend's father-in-law, Jack, likes to tell the story of how he got his first job. He needed summer employment to help pay for his college tuition, but he didn't have any of the qualifications necessary for the jobs that were open. Finally after a week of fruitless searching, he walked into the office of a large lumberyard and applied for the position of assistant manager. He was only twenty-one years old with zero training, no letters of recommendation, and the only work experience he had prior was labor on his father's farm.

"But," he told the manager, "I'm willing to come here every day for two weeks and work for you for free. You don't have to pay me a thing. But at the end of two weeks, if you find my services valuable, well then, you have to offer me the job and pay me for those two weeks."

The manager took Jack up on his offer. They shook hands, and Jack went home.

The next day Jack showed up at that lumberyard raring to go. For two weeks he was the first one to arrive in the morning and the last one to leave. He ran around so much, his shirts were soaked through with sweat by the end of the day. It was his goal to make himself so valuable, the boss would wonder what he'd ever done without him

By the end of those two weeks, Jack had himself a job. He kept that job and worked his way through college. He was making more money and in a higher position than guys who had been at the lumber yard ten years or more. But Jack had been willing to do the hard first. He went on to graduate with a degree in business. Later in life, Jack became the president of his own commercial real estate company. Jack just turned seventy-one this year, and he isn't quite ready to retire.

"Retire? Why would I retire?" he says. "The way I have things set up now, everybody else does all the work for me. All I have to do is show up on the golf course a few days a week."

The habit of practicing Hard Easy is the one underlying success habits that no one is talking about. It is a discipline that, once developed, takes care of itself. In fact, creating favorable conditions, thinking win/win, and paying the price up front will all become second nature. You won't even have to think about it. Start doing them and you will immediately see good things coming back to you. Develop the habit of doing them regularly, and the good will compound. You will experience a life in flow, paving the way for a complete and successful RichLife.

There is a chart in your Action Guide found at www .RichLifeActionGuide.com that shows the process of applying the Hard Easy principle. Notice that at the beginning, you might feel as if you are moving against gravity. Developing a discipline is hard for everybody at first. It might be made even harder if it is an area of particular challenge to you. But carry on, even if at first it seems all up hill. Stay with it. You will reach the peak.

HAITI THEN AND NOW

Back in the 1980s, the poorest country in the Western Hemisphere was under the rule of dictator Jean-Claude Duvalier, a man who came to power at the young age of nineteen. The majority of his people lived on less than $2 a day in a country with a history of natural disasters. The island sits on a strike-slip fault system at the merger of two branches—the Septentrional-Oriente fault in the north and the Enriquillo-Plantain Garden fault in the south. The question of a catastrophic earthquake was not one of *if*, but one of *when*. For years, studies pointed to the gathering stress of these faults and a major risk of seismic activity in Haiti's capitol city of Port-au-Prince. Scientists published articles and presented data. Global concern was also expressed over the country's ability to handle an emergency of any magnitude given the limitations of their emergency services. A country with no building codes, it was recommended to rebuild the infrastructure of Port-au-Prince using better technology as was done in the city of San Francisco. Over 2 million dollars of foreign aid came pouring in.

Duvalier had the funds, but rebuilding the capitol of Port-au-Prince no doubt seemed like a daunting job. No action was taken. No rebuilding was done. In 1986 the dictator left his country after being ousted, going into exile, and allegedly taking the country's treasury with him.

On Tuesday, January 12, 2010, an earthquake of catastrophic magnitude hit Haiti roughly sixteen miles west of its capitol city. Because of the shallow depth of the quake, the damage was devastating. Over 30,000 commercial buildings collapsed, burying hundreds of thousands of people under the rubble. Over 250,000 residences were demolished, displacing more than 1 million people. The entire education system was destroyed as well as land and sea transport and all hospitals in the capitol; relief and recovery came to a standstill. One year after the quake, only 5 percent of the rubble had been cleared and no rebuilding had begun. The death toll was estimated to be over 200,000 and there were more than 300,000 injured. Outbreaks of cholera continue, accounting for more than 50 percent of the world's total cases, and over 200,000 people continue to be displaced.

IT'S COMING

A disaster on this scale is more than most of us can wrap our heads around. Unless we've had the opportunity to visit Haiti, we can only imagine—from pictures and reports—what these people were and are still going through. One hopes Duvalier is experiencing remorse for his actions; one hopes for justice.

It's interesting to note that in September of 2007, after more than twenty years of quiet displacement, Duvalier did make a radio broadcast to the people of Haiti. In this broadcast, he apologized and afterward returned to Haiti where he was immediately arrested. Of course by then, for the people of Haiti, it was too late. The task of rebuilding the infrastructure of an entire city is an enormous and expensive job. But had they done it back in the eighties, it would have merely been *hard* compared with what the country is facing now. What's hard compared to devastating? What's hard compared to millions of displaced families and hundreds of thousands dead?

In the end, what it comes down to is every man's own conscience. We are taking a look at the micro/macro idea with regard to our actions. This is what I mean by Hard Easy—when you make the easy decisions today, you endure a much harder future. The examples on a national scale are numerous. Closer to home, we have the devastation of Hurricane Katrina in New Orleans after the city failed to strengthen its levees when they had the chance. In business we have the BP oil spill and its lack of redundant safety measures. It's easy to point the finger at these examples and shake our heads. It's easy to see where they went wrong. What I am asking you to do now is to take this in on a much smaller, more personal scale. I am asking you to do the hard work of looking within.

For all of us, it's coming. We may not want to admit it. We may not want to think about it. But *your life* is here, waiting for you to step up. You are the only person who knows whether or not you are living the life you are meant to live. You are the only person who knows whether or not you are fulfilled. You are also the only one who can do anything about it. The day will come when you realize you are out of time. That day will either be one of peaceful surrender, or it will be like that of a seismic quake. If you are lucky, you may survive and be "awakened" by your personal disaster into realizing *Hey, it's not too late!* You can start to change things. You can begin by practicing the Hard Easy principle:

> Every day you face important decisions. Commit to doing the hard things first, and the rest of your life will come easy. Conversely, doing the easy things now makes the rest of life hard.

Invest up front in the things that are important to you. These are all the things we have talked about including meaningful work, time with loved ones, and our own good health. Do the hard now. There is always a choice. You can invest, paying the price, or you can wait and do nothing, then later pay the cost.

PAYING THE PRICE OR PAYING THE COST

Most people when given the choice will do the easy thing first. They reason: if it's going to be hard either now or later, well then

I'll pick later! They would rather deal with it when it happens. After all, they think, why do today what you can put off until tomorrow?

This is the kind of thinking that leads to national disasters.

Let me put it to you another way. Let's talk money.

On April 20, 2010, more than four million barrels of oil spilled into the Gulf of Mexico after the Deepwater Horizon rig exploded. Eleven workers were killed and millions more gallons of oil continued to flow for three months until the well was finally capped on July 15th.

In looking to the cause of the accident, experts debated the safety of drilling for oil offshore. Backup systems and redundant safety measures required by U.S. regulations have been reported as weaker than those of other countries. These safety measures cost money, and it was argued that the possibility exists they are not worth their price tag.

What is the estimated *price* tag of implementing stricter safety regulations? *$500,000.*

What is the *cost* of damages to the ecosystems on which we depend, the *cost* of livelihoods and loss of lives, the *cost* of the largest oil spill in U.S. history? *$40 billion.*

Which is greater, the price or the cost?

The "hard" that comes later is not the same as the "hard" that comes now. We saw that in our example with the people of Haiti. It would have been a lot of work to rebuild the infrastructure of Port-au-Prince back in the 1980s. I'm sure it seemed like a huge amount of money to invest. But compared to what they faced later with nowhere to even put the rubble and hundreds of thousands of lives lost, the price would have been small in comparison. When you fail to pay the *price* up front—the price of sound infrastructure, the price of stronger levees, the price of safety—the *cost* in the end is significantly more.

They say an ounce of prevention is worth a pound of cure. The price up front might seem like a lot to pay. But think about the numbers. You're going to pay one way or another. This is true in business and in life. This is true of the small personal decisions we make as well as the large ones. This is the difference between micro and macroeconomics, the difference between a poor and a rich life.

Learning to forge the discipline required to pay the price up front is uncomfortable. Paying for tuition or life insurance, exercising, time management and visits with family, consistent marketing, prospecting, and referral gathering can all be uncomfortable at times. But what are the costs and consequences of *not* doing these things? You will most certainly experience feelings of frustration, disappointment, scarcity, fear, doubt, worry, sleepless nights, self-loathing, stress, and possible illness and/or death.

By *not* practicing Hard Easy, the hard in the end will be worse. It might seem hard at first, but really the only thing more difficult than Hard Easy is *not* practicing it! In other words, the energy you spend being afraid and feeling bad about *not* doing what needs to be done often exceeds the reality of what it takes to just go and do it.

By practicing Hard Easy, you will do the hard thing first, take into account the big picture of the whole, and do what you know in your heart to be right. This principle when applied to each of the 10 Investments will set you on your way toward your RichLife.

By now you have made some decisions. You also have a clear path to follow and a few key guiding principles. But there's one more little thing I'm going to let you in on, one more thing to keep in the back of your mind: It almost never works out the way you plan it.

TOM CORLEY AND UNINTENDED CONSEQUENCES

After ten years of doing hard things—researching, writing, and promoting his book, *Rich Habits*—author Tom Corley was ready to give up. His low point came during the two-year period between

2010 and 2011, when Tom worked relentlessly three hours a day, every day, pitching, posting, and tweeting to the media, trying to get publicity and attention for his book.

> The only thing I got was an article in New Jersey's largest newspaper, *The Star Ledger*. Later that week I sold 200 or so books, but that didn't seem like a lot of books for such a great article. I was downcast and depressed. That led to a couple months of inactivity.

One unintended consequence of his initial failure to promote the *Rich Habits* book was the writing and promotion of his second and third books, including the eBook called *The Top 100 Cheapest Places to Retire in the U.S.* Explains Tom:

> When you are working with a publisher, it can take up to 18 months to get the book out in print. Because the content I was working with for these new books needed to remain current, I decided to take the digital route. I created, copy wrote, and learned how to pitch the media. I failed with the *Rich Habits* book, but shifting gears and going through the process of creating those two eBooks gave me new insight and experience. The light bulb went off, so to speak.

Tom got media attention in various newspapers across the country, which in turn landed him a spot on regional TV in his home state of New Jersey. That led to his first Internet television show, an interview with AOL, during which he sold over 7,000 eBooks in just half an hour. After that, Tom started doing as many interviews for his eBooks as he could.

It had been about three or four months since he had done anything with his *Rich Habits* book when Tom received the emails.

There were two emails, written by readers from two different parts of the country. Both readers expressed how the *Rich Habits* book had changed their lives for the better. They also both told him that his book reminded them of a book called *The Wealthy Barber*, only it was better.

Curious, Tom did a little research and found that *The Wealthy Barber* written by David Chilton had sold over 2.5 million copies. And he thought, *Wow, why can't I sell 2.5 million copies of* Rich Habits? In a moment of gutsy brio, Tom contacted David Chilton and forwarded the emails, pointing out that here were two readers who said that *Rich Habits* was a better book, so why couldn't his book get any attention?

David Chilton called Tom within five minutes of receiving the email.

"It doesn't matter if your book is good or great," explained David. "It just has to be good enough. What really matters is conquering the media." He defined what the media was—television, radio, the Internet, and print. "You can't conquer only one or two. You have to conquer all four."

David recommended that Tom read *1001 Ways to Market Your Book*, by John Kremer, and even though Tom had already read it, he went back and read it again. Over the course of the next six months, Tom did 150 radio interviews and perfected the craft of pitching and being interviewed by the media. During a local show in Minneapolis, he got the attention of the show's host and publicist, Lauri Flaquer, who later called him up and said, "You're great, and I'm going to be your publicist whether you like it or not." This was in February of 2013. Tom did what she told him to do, and one of his tweets got picked up by Farnoosh Torabi of the Yahoo! Finance show *Financially Fit*, at that time known as the most-watched personal finance show on the Internet. Her crew came down from their plush Manhattan office to Rahway, New Jersey for the taping. On July 16, 2013, his first *Financially Fit* piece was released.

The interview went viral.

One of the 2.2 million hits that day was media great Dave Ramsey. The Dave Ramsey show broadcasts on over 500 radio stations from coast to coast and attracts more than 8 million listeners. That night Tom was working late with a client, and when he walked in the door at 9:30, his wife said to him, "Some guy named Dave Ramsey has been trying to get a hold of you."

"Dave Ramsey?" Tom was surprised. "Why is Dave Ramsey trying to reach me?"

"Your Yahoo interview. He was talking about you all day."

Tom's publicist also called that night to tell him that *Rich Habits* was #1 out of all the books on Amazon. Tom logged on to see for himself, and sure enough, there was his book, ahead of five or six New York Times bestsellers. Two days later he was interviewed on the Dave Ramsey show, and *Rich Habits* stayed in the top 100 list for a month. During that time, he sold over 13,000 books.

"I guess the lesson I learned is that persistence is the key to success," says Tom. "But David Chilton said it best when he asked me, 'Do you love your book?' And I said yes, it's one of the greatest books I've ever read. Then he said, 'You don't need to convince me. Convince yourself. If you think it's great, pursue it, and don't give up until the day you die.'"

LIKE SNOWFLAKES ON A MOUNTAIN

When Tom originally set out to write and publish *Rich Habits*, he had hopes and expectations about how things should progress. When things didn't go according to plan, as often they don't, Tom went through a bit of a struggle. But what makes Tom's story different is what he did next: Tom kept pushing that bolder up the hill. He kept learning, kept searching, kept asking, *What am I doing wrong?* What could I be doing better? And what is that successful guy doing that I'm not?

Oftentimes when you are pursuing a major goal or dream, unintended consequences occur. These are things that you could never predict, wouldn't expect, things not even on your radar. The first unintended consequence was the success of his eBooks, followed by the interest from a publicist, and the interview that went viral. These are things that just started to show up, one after another, by the virtue of Tom's persistence.

"You feel like you are continuously pushing the boulder up the hill," says Tom. "But doing these things every day is like snowflakes that land on the side of a mountain. You don't really notice them until all of a sudden, you have an unintended consequence that leads to or becomes a small avalanche of success."

Tom is still hoping for the big avalanche to occur. He still does things every day to promote his book. "I call it my daily five," says Tom, "and the only exceptions to this are the days when we have a family event or family vacation. It sounds like work but it's not. *When you have something you are passionate about, it's not work.*"

THE ART OF TACKING

A friend of mine likes to compare the way in which people move through life to boats. He says there are two personality types—the motorboat people and the sailboat people. Motorboat people go from point A to point B in a relatively straight line. If they have a problem, they power through it. They do it the way they've always done it, by revving up the engine. When the engine breaks, they fix it or get a new one.

The sailboat people are on more of a journey. They rely on the wind and their ability to tack, to change the position of the sails, so they can effectively harness the breeze. They work with the elements around them in a kind of dance. They are constantly making little adjustments as they go along over the water, and that's the beauty of it. The art of tacking is what they find so exhilarating about the sail.

Tacking is defined as the act of changing from one position or direction to another. Sometimes in life, we need to tack, to make an adjustment. Tom Corley altered his course and wrote an eBook, then adjusted the way he pitched the media. Altering our course of action just slightly is sometimes all that is needed to optimize attainment of our goal. Sometimes, even our goals change. I invite you to welcome this as part of the journey. In my own life, I have found the times of the greatest change to be when I learned the most. If you get the adjustment wrong, well then, you have an opportunity to rise to the challenge. You have a chance to raise or lower your sails.

Getting it right feels good, too, but keep in mind that your RichLife encompasses the journey.

IN FLOW

Once the Hard Easy becomes habit and a way of life, the easy also becomes a way of life. You live in a place of flow, where everything that happens is perfect, a part of the plan, a place of no struggle. The deadline has been moved? Perfect. The flight is delayed? Perfect.

My friend likes to tell the story of a flight he experienced at an airport in Washington when coming home from a business trip. There he was sitting comfortably in his assigned seat, everyone buckled and all the baggage stowed, the plane waiting on the runway. All of a sudden, the cabin begins to fill with smoke. An announcement comes on over the speaker system, "Do not grab your bags; do not grab your coats. *Get off the plane.*"

Imagine thirty-five people standing out on a runway with big planes roaring by. It was winter and they were freezing cold without their coats. Neither did they have any of their belongings.

Grumbling began to ensue. But my friend took one look around and said, "Well, here's the good news. They found the problem now, before we were up in the air."

Everybody quieted down.

When you are in flow, nothing is a problem. You have the ability to tack and change, to deal with the wind and change direction. You put into practice the habit of Hard Easy, so you already did all of the things in your control to attain a favorable outcome. Now you can enjoy what comes and make adjustments as necessary. In the end, you realize that any problems that crop up, like a delayed airplane for example, were in the end necessary to things going your way.

In a New Position

I talked about my early years as a financial planner just starting out, when I spent countless hours dialing for dollars. I would like to share with you where I am today. I now enjoy a growing financial planning business, a regular radio show, and a series of coaching programs that have a waiting list. I meet regularly with a select number of clients for lunch or for coffee, and I share in their dreams and experiences. I have developed some wonderful relationships. The RichLife message is attracting the perfect clients to me. This is the Holy Grail of financial planning and really of any profession—to be the one who is sought out as opposed to having to hunt down work every day.

This is where we are leading you, but it won't happen for you unless you are willing to do the hard first. I would never have gotten to where I am now if I had not made myself sit down and make those cold calls every day. Tom Corley would not have topped the Amazon bestseller list had he not persisted with his daily five. Do the hard first, and the easy will follow. The work will become habit and success inevitable.

BREAKING THE INERTIA

We have talked throughout this book about fear and breaking out of the scarcity mentality many of us are stuck in. Because this chapter is about a principle that requires *action*, I'd like to spend a minute talking about *inertia*.

Inertia comes from the Latin word for idleness and in physics defines the tendency of a resting body to resist motion. We naturally resist change. On a spiritual level, inertia is fear mode. Break out of that and you have the beginning of wisdom. There is a part of you that knows you're here to do something. But most of us become paralyzed by our fear instead of taking action. We fall into patterns.

Another definition of inertia states that a body moving in a straight line will continue going in a straight line. If you feel that you have found your area of life purpose but still haven't fully realized your niche, it might be time to break out of old patterns. It might be time to make an inner shift.

In my own life story, there was an important shift that I had to make in order to get where I am today. There came a point after eight years of working hard as a financial planner where I realized I wanted more. I had established a client base I was proud of. While I still made calls, I was no longer dependent on them for my gas money, so to speak. But it was starting to feel like a grind. As I described in an earlier chapter, the things I enjoyed about being a financial planner were not occurring enough and I was still stuck in the mode of crunching through the numbers.

After meeting with Richard, the miserable multimillionaire, my eyes were opened. The realization that life was about more than money propelled me toward my real mission. I wanted to be more than just a financial planner who helped people find the best mutual fund. I wanted to really help people utilize their assets and resources to achieve their definition of a RichLife. But at the beginning, I didn't know how to bridge the two.

I started with what I considered little experiments. Little tests. I began with the clients I was most comfortable with, those with whom I had a history and felt safe, and I started asking them more personal questions. I found that when I approached them from the authentic place of really wanting to help, wanting to add value to their lives, the connection was much stronger. My relationship with these clients started to grow. I was able to offer a more complete service, and as more and more of these little experiments became successes, I became bolder to the point where I now speak about living a RichLife regularly on radio shows, online and offline media, seminars, and live training sessions.

My focus has shifted from making a living to adding value to the lives of my clients—from just selling my clients products to *serving* my clients. I now enjoy a career that dovetails my knowledge of financial planning *and* my love for helping other people. This, for me, is my definition of a RichLife.

GIVE ANYTHING

A lot of people say it. Maybe you've even said it yourself. *I'd give anything to have what that person has, be where that person is, do what that person is doing.* Is this true? Would you really give anything?

No, of course you wouldn't. And by now you realize that you shouldn't. Success must be measured in terms of what was given up in order to attain it. Monetary success is only one small part of the RichLife picture. So what do you have to give up in order to achieve the RichLife picture? I'll tell you.

What you'll have to give up is your fear, your laziness, your inertia, and your procrastination. Instead of saying, "I'll give anything to have that job," you can say, "I'm willing to give up my fear, my laziness, my inertia, and my procrastination in order to have that job." That's all you'll have to give up. That's as hard as the Hard

Easy gets. And in my experience, the worst part of the fear comes just before the actual doing. As evidenced by Tom Corely, once you get to the doing part, it already becomes easier because you are absorbed in a task. You will also find that other forces and unintended consequences come into play once you've discovered your life purpose and are set into motion. Help comes from unexpected places, and as you tack and make adjustments, you'll soon experience days of smooth sailing, or at least moments of them.

Yes, the hard requires effort from you. Yes, it requires that you give up a few things. But it does not require that you suffer. The suffering of *not* doing is much greater, I can assure you.

I first saw success when I started applying the principle of Hard Easy. I developed a discipline, made it a habit, and then took it to the next level. Taking it the next level required an inner shift. It required that I give up my fear and inertia. It required that I work to add value to the lives of others instead of merely adding to my own income and accumulating stuff.

This inner shift was the most important part of shifting me out of my old patterns.

At first, I was like a deer out on the ice. But I started small, with little experiments, until I eventually became more and more comfortable with my new legs. The more I live and work this way, the more I meet other people who are doing the same thing, applying the same principles in their own chosen fields.

SERVANT LEADERSHIP

I had a doctor call in to my radio show one day. After speaking to her for just a few minutes, we both had the realization that we were doing the same thing. When she treats her patients, she asks them about *everything*—their home life, their jobs, even their relationships. She takes a holistic approach to health in the same way I approach financial planning. By doing this, she is able to create the conditions most favorable to really helping them.

That doctor is a servant to her patients just as I am a servant to my clients. We serve them, and this creates the ultimate dynamic. Forget about the negative images you might have of servants or slaves. The idea of offering service to others first is a shift that goes to the heart of creating a RichLife. It embodies all the principles we have talked about. By being a good steward to your clients, your patients, your guests, and by treating all the people in your professional life this way, you set up a dynamic where everybody is serving each other and everybody wins.

Imagine if your boss had this attitude toward you at your place of employment. What if you were constantly getting the message from her that *she* was there to serve *you*? Not only was she *paying* you to do your job, but she made sure you had the tools you needed to get the job done. Imagine how that would increase your productivity. Imagine how that would benefit the customers *you* were serving. The ripple effects would be far reaching, indeed. This is how we change the world.

Do the hard first in the spirit of service to others and you will be amazed at the far-reaching rewards. This one Master Investment applied alone to any situation has the potential to bring about the most good. Master it, and you are on your way toward having it easy and toward living your RichLife.

 ## PORTFOLIO BUILDER

Whatever it is that you want to do or become, tackle the hard first. Make it a discipline, and develop the habit. Everybody wants to have life easy. Few people are willing to do what it takes to get that easy life. What choice will you make?

> **Do the hard now, and
> the easy will follow.**

Make the decision to pay the price up front, and you'll have a sound structure that in the end will cost you less. Take this one step further and apply it to the way you treat others—employees, friends, and family.

THE TAKE-AWAYS

- In most everything in life, in order to be successful, you've got to work hard up front.

- To push past the dread, make the doing a habit.

- When you fail to pay the *price* up front—the price of sound infrastructure, the price of stronger levees, the price of safety—the *cost* in the end is significantly more.

- Every day you face important decisions. Commit to doing the hard things first, and the rest will come *easy*. Conversely, doing the easy first makes the rest of life hard.

ACTION STEPS

- Choose one discipline in either your personal or professional life that you are currently not doing, but that by doing could make a greater difference. For example: *I commit to the discipline of booking one new client meeting daily.*

- Divide a piece of paper in two columns; on the left-hand column write *The Price of Hard Easy*; on the right-hand column write *The Cost of Easy Hard.*

➤ Start with *The Price of Hard Easy*. Write down every hard thing about the new discipline, including any negative thought that could possibly arise while doing the new hard thing. These negative thoughts can include anything that runs through your mind when you imagine yourself undertaking your new discipline (e.g., booking one new client meeting daily). It is important to be thorough with this section. Take your time and really extract every potentially unpleasant thought or feeling that may exist on or beneath the surface with being disciplined in this area. Do not move on until you have at least seven things listed. Expect that some of them will be big and some of them silly. For example:

The Price of Hard Easy

1. Having to stay later at work.

2. Taking time away from family or friends.

3. Fear of getting hung up on or yelled at.

4. Experiencing nervousness about meeting someone new.

5. Having to invest in some nicer clothes.

6. Uncertainty about whether or not I'll be able to keep it up.

7. Wondering if it will be worth it.

➤ Now move over to *The Cost of Easy Hard*. The things you'll write down here are best seen as the consequences of doing the easy thing. These are the negative results you are certain will occur if you fail to commit to your new discipline (e.g., booking one new client meeting daily). Don't be gentle here. Be authentic with the harsh truth of what will happen to your business, your family, self-esteem, lifestyle, health, or retirement if you take the easy path. What regrets and consequences would you have?

The Cost of Easy Hard

1. Feeling like my business is progressively sinking.

2. Increased stress because I'm not generating enough income.

3. Poor self-esteem.

4. Getting home early and having too much to drink because I feel lousy about my day.

5. Envy of the success of others.

6. Feeling like I'm not setting a good example for my kids.

7. Missing out on a better quality of life.

   - Which column contains things that are unacceptable and far more painful?

   - What realizations have you had as a result of this exercise?

   - **Download** your free copy of the Action Guide for *The RichLife: Ten Investments for True Wealth* at www.RichLifeActionGuide.com.

FINAL THOUGHTS

"Life is constantly providing us with new
funds. New resources. Even when we are
reduced to mobility. In life's ledger there
is no such thing as frozen assets."
—HENRY MILLER, American author (1891-1980)

DEFINING YOUR RICHLIFE

As you have journeyed through this book, I trust that your eyes
have been opened and the lens through which you view money
has been cleared. I suspect that new thoughts and ideas have been
growing in your mind. And if you have read this far in the book, I
also believe that you are ready to take action. You've probably been
envisioning your own RichLife—what you'd like to be doing and
the people you'd like to be doing it with. No doubt you have been
wondering—maybe even planning—how to get from where you are
now to where you want to be.

The RichLife: Ten Investments for True Wealth has been designed to change you, to adjust your thinking, and to challenge your ideas and perceptions. If you previously thought that money was the answer to all your problems, hopefully you have now come to realize that money is not, and never will be, the *end-all answer* to living your RichLife. It does, however, play an important part. Money in of itself has no value until it is utilized. The best applications are those where money is used to serve. With a focus on utilization, money then becomes a tool, as it was meant to be, and not the master.

The world likes to tell us that financial security lies in something or someone outside of us. I hope that belief is changing. Of all the assets, physical, financial, and human, *you are the most important asset you have.* Those who ascribe to the RichLife philosophy are not focused on retirement or how much they will need to get along in their later years. They are focused on discovering and living out their life purpose, on serving and contributing the most value to their loved ones and to the world in which they live.

If you have not yet discovered your RichLife, don't wait another minute. Start with the life-changing question mentioned in Investment #2: *If you could spend your days doing what you love whether or not you received monetary compensation, what would you do?*

Next, ask yourself that sobering question that appeared in Investment #5: *If you had great health and enjoyed all the normal physical capabilities, and yet you knew you had exactly six months to live, what would you be doing?*

Take the time to complete the action exercises laid out for you in the book, particularly those in Investment #2. You can also find the complete set of action exercises on my website. They are collated in a workbook titled, *The RichLife 10 Investments Action Guide*, and it's yours free to download and share with others at www.RichLifeActionGuide.com. Answer the questions in this action guide (or at the end of these chapters) and begin applying the master principle of Hard Easy. These tools were designed specifically to help you build the bridge from where you are now to where you want to be. To help you imagine the bridge to your RichLife, we carry the analogy one step further.

BUILDING YOUR BRIDGE

There are three main components to a bridge, all of them equally important—the superstructure, sub-structure, and foundation supports.

The superstructure is the road surface—that part of the bridge where vehicles and pedestrians pass over. We can think of this as the superhighway of life where the day to day plays out. This is where important decisions are made in the moment—turn left, turn right, deal or no deal.

The foundation supports lie underneath. They are set into place first, and as their name suggests, they bear the weight of everything built on top. These supports are responsible for the overall weakness or strength of the bridge, for its duration and its ability to span distance. It is also the part of the bridge you don't see. Like the roots to a tree, these drilled shaft or pipe caps are underground or underwater where they provide sustenance, if you will, to the entire structure. When applied to our RichLife, we can think of these foundation supports as the 10 investments or principles we've been talking about—stewardship, life purpose, viewing life as a school, building relationships, creating experiences, mastering your money map, understanding risk transfer, building your team, health, and contribution.

Most people don't see the work that goes into building these supports, but they do see the results. The secret to a strong bridge is its foundation. The stronger the foundation, the more secure the bridge, and the farther in life it can take you.

But the third component, the sub-structure, is what really makes the difference between achieving or not achieving your RichLife. It's the difference between the people who have it all and those who spend their life wanting. It's the difference between hoping and doing, the difference between staying stuck and moving forward.

The sub-structure of a bridge is basically the layer between the top and the bottom. In our RichLife, this in-between layer is the guiding principle that dictates the success of our daily decisions and the strength of the investments made below ground. This is the Master Investment—the principle of Hard Easy.

This principle applied to just one single area of your life has the potential to unlock the greatest change. Without it, the surface of your life may look okay for a while, but eventually over time it will erode and crumble. Without the redundant supports of the 10 investments we talked about, the bridge, over time, will collapse.

To build your bridge to get you from here to there requires an even development of all three areas. You have the tools. Let's get building!

GROW YOUR RICHLIFE PORTFOLIO

By working through the Portfolio Builder and Action Step activities throughout the book, you are well on your way toward the creation of your RichLife. Now it's time to put those investments together and grow your RichLife portfolio. Whenever one thinks about investing, the common term that comes to mind is an investment portfolio. This refers to the different types of asset classes that make up your investment strategy such as large or small company stocks, bonds, real estate, precious metals, private businesses, etc. Likewise, I have drawn an analogy to move you toward investing in your RichLife with what I call your *RichLife Portfolio.*

The design and creation of your RichLife Portfolio will provide you with a visual guide. It will show you in which areas you are weak and need more supports; conversely, it will reveal your strengths. You can begin by downloading the diagram by visiting www.RichLifeActionGuide.com to download your free RichLife Action Guide where you can print up your own Portfolio template.

Like a financial plan, your RichLife Portfolio is an investment in your future. It is a tool to help you get from where you are now to where you want to go. It's also very personal. It won't look like anybody else's.

The first exercise I take my coaching clients through starts with a pie chart. Designed to grow like the rings of a tree, the investment called *Your RichLife* is divided into eight main areas:

1. Physical—your body, appearance, health, and mental state. We devoted an entire chapter to this, your primary asset.

2. Spiritual—your faith, faults, self-love, appreciation, and gratitude. Not everyone has a religion they believe in, but everyone has faith in something. These are the principles that you live by, your guiding counsel. This is what dictates the way you behave and the kind of person you become.

3. Financial—your savings, debt, credit scores, and income goals. Money is the vehicle to help you get from here to there. It is meant to serve you.

4. Relationships—your family, friends, acquaintances, professional relationships and networking goals. We also spent a chapter on this important investment.

5. Environments—your spaces such as workspace, home, car, time in nature, community, house of worship, and neighborhood. This is important to

consider, because many people live or work in spaces that are detrimental to getting anything done. Our environments also require good stewardship.

6.   Fun and Recreation—your hobbies, free time preferences, relaxation, and travel goals. This is what you do for enjoyment. These are the times you build lasting memories. Sometimes it can also give you clues to your life purpose.

7.   Professional—your business, career, or job. Being a stay-at-home parent can very well be your current life purpose. This is what you love to do and how you offer value to the world. These are goals such as getting promoted, attaining clients, receiving a raise, or helping someone to succeed. There may be temporary jobs you don't mind doing that help bridge you from where you are to where you want to go.

8.   Legacy—contribution to the world, gifts to charity and community, your mark. This is what you want your epitaph to say, what makes your heart sing, the bigger picture of what you want your life to stand for. There can be multiple components. Examples: I want to have x amount of dollars to leave behind for a charity; I want to give my three girls confidence and basic know-how to succeed in life; I want my son to be proud to call me Dad; I want to write a book that can help thousands; I want to contribute to the elimination of poverty; I want to cure cancer.

COLOR YOUR RINGS

RichLife Portfolio Courtesy of The Success Coach Institute ©2010

In the RichLife portfolio diagram found in your Action Guide, give yourself a visual of where you are in each of these eight areas by coloring in the appropriate "rings" with 1 being the lowest and 10 being the highest. The ultimate goal is to have the same number of rings colored in each area because even growth across all areas is necessary to the achievement of a balanced RichLife. Think of your RichLife Portfolio as the wheel of a bike. If too much weight sits in any one area, the ride will be bumpy and potentially treacherous. So, too, will your day-to-day life. And as with any investment portfolio, you never want to put all your eggs in one basket.

In the RichLife Portfolio diagram, the master principle of Hard Easy sits in the middle of the circle. The Investments we talked about are vehicles that can move you toward your RichLife. Practicing the principle of Hard Easy is the magic key that will get any vehicle started.

CHOOSE THREE

Next we have our coaching clients choose three areas in their life that need attention. Using the analogy of a bicycle wheel, it should be apparent to you which areas require your attention. If all the areas are evenly matched, good for you! You can select three areas to begin growth.

Keep in mind the process is a lot like playing monopoly. When you own all three of any property, you are allowed to "build." But the rules of the game require you build evenly, never adding more than one house at a time on any single property within your block of three. In the game of Monopoly, you build your houses as evenly as your monopoly money budget allows. This is exactly how you want to set about growing your RichLife Portfolio. You will need to balance your assets and budget your time to find the ideal asset allocation that works for you

Now that you have become familiar with all of the investment concepts and chosen your three areas, the next thing is to step out and take action.

STEPPING OUT

I recommend designating a RichLife notebook where you can chart your own personal journey. In your notebook, make a list of the actions you intend to take. Say you have chosen the following three areas to improve—physical, financial, and environment.

A good place to begin is with the first investment of wise stewardship. Apply this investment to each of the three areas and take action by doing the Hard first.

In terms of your physical body, commit to doing one thing every week that will result in positive change over the long term. For example, sign up for a yoga class, join a gym, or set the alarm one hour earlier and go for a morning walk. Choose something that fits into your lifestyle and is realistic for you. You will do the Hard first, getting up earlier or stopping work and going to the gym or to your class. It will get easier as the hard becomes habit, and then as you start seeing positive physical results it will become easier still.

Oftentimes, areas overlap. You might find a friend to join you on those walks and the time then becomes both an investment in your health and in the growth of that relationship. The walks and the times you have together will, over time, create memories, adding even more to your RichLife.

At the same time you are doing this, begin a practice of wise stewardship in the area of your finances and the environments you live in. Perhaps you start a savings account, paying yourself first by deducting $25 a paycheck. Maybe you buy a plant for your office. Maybe you use the accumulated savings to finally rebuild the deck that is falling apart. Or maybe it's an investment of your time— creating a balance sheet and income statement with your partner, cleaning out the garage, having a sale, or donating items you no longer need to charity.

RICHLIFE RESOURCES

A successful life is built over time, not in one day, with consistent and regular investments. If you get stuck, refer back to the chapters. Take a look at one of the 10 investments and apply the appropriate principle. For example, you might use the principle of wise stewardship to improve your surroundings. After a period of ninety days, take a look at that area in your life portfolio, and give yourself another ring in your RichLife Portfolio if you have seen growth or improvement. It's important to check in regularly and give yourself a pat on the back when you've earned it, especially at first. As the hard gets easier and the benefits begin compounding, the unfolding of your RichLife will become its own reward.

Meanwhile visit my website www.BeauHenderson.com and take advantage of resources such as the "True Wealth" weekly newsletter, archives, and station listings of *The RichLife Show* and educational events. I personally invite you to join over 70,000 friends in our growing community of people committed to living their definition of a RichLife.

SHARE YOUR STORY

Nothing could be more beneficial to the world we live in than for each one of us to fully realize and achieve our RichLife. As Steve D'Annunzio points out, the unintentional consequence of not discovering and living your life purpose is that problems specific to your unique gifting and talents go unsolved. This is why you see billions of problems existing on our planet. Becoming aware of and living out your life purpose is more than just the beginning of self-fulfillment, it is a personal and moral responsibility. By living this way, you make a significant difference to the world in which we live.

As I said at the beginning of this book, this is a dialog and we want to hear from you. How have the RichLife concepts changed your life? What kind of difference has incorporating them made to you and your family? Join the RichLife international community that includes the voices you have heard throughout this book. Step up and take the RichLife challenge by sharing your own story. Our top stories will be entered to win personalized coaching and products designed to help you live your RichLife. Join the ranks of Maggie Munyua, Yudy Cid, Sussil Liyanage, Corey Jahnke, Kyle Wilson, Bob Burg, Nishangan Thiyagarajah, Vicki Moore, and Tom Corley, and share your story with others who will in turn be encouraged by your successes, trials, and valuable lessons. Adding value to the lives of others will in turn bless you as the circle of giving continues to give back.

Share your story at www.BeauHenderson.com.

Sharing with others the life lessons that I have learned is a big part of my RichLife. It's also one of the ways I choose to add value to the world around me. To the thousands of clients who have shared their life lessons and passed down their wisdom, I am forever grateful. To those of you encountering this philosophy for the first time, I thank you for taking this journey with me and becoming part of my RichLife. I pray that reading *The RichLife: Ten Investments for True Wealth* has provided a rich experience for you.

To your RichLife,
BEAU HENDERSON

BIBLIOGRAPHY

Armstrong, Karen. *Through the Narrow Gate.* New York: St. Martin's Press, 1981. Introduction the Second Edition, 1994.

What the Bleep Do We Know? Directed by William Arntz, Betsy Chasse, and Mark Vincente. Beverly Hills, CA: 20th Century Fox, 2004. DVD.

Carter-Scott, Chérie. *If Life Is a Game, These Are the Rules.* New York: Broadway Books, 1998.

Chapin, Harry. "Cat's in the Cradle," *Verities & Balderdash*, Elektra, 1974, CD.

Cialdini, Robert B. *The Psychology of Persuasion.* Allyn and Bacon. 2001.

Covey, Stephen R. *The 7 Habits of Highly Effective People.* New York: Fireside, 1990.

Coelho, Paulo. *The Alchemist.* New York: Harper Collins, 2006.

D'Annunzio, Steven. *The Prosperity Paradigm.* New York: White Light Press, 2006.

Hawkins, Dr. David. Power vs. Force: The Hidden Determinants of Human Behavior. Carlsbad: Hay House, 2002.

Rosenbaum, Andrew. *The Wealth Swing Coach.* Mercury Print, USA, 2009.

Soul Purpose Institute, *Ultimate Stewardship Workbook.* Facilitated by Steve D' Annunzio. Mercury Print, USA, 2009.

Nicholson, Jodi. Success Coach Institute, *iCoach To Success System.* New York: Sterling Publishing Group, 2010.

Tolle, Eckhart. *A New Earth: Awakening to Your Life's Purpose.* New York: A Plume Book, Penguin Group, 2006.

Websites

Armstrong, Karen. *Twelve Steps to a Compassionate Life*, Dec. 27, 2011. From the Charter for Compassion website: http://www.charterforcompassion.org.

"What the Bleep Do We Know!?" Article based off movie released in 2004 and directed by William Arntz, Mark Vicente, and Betsy Chasse. Website: http://www.Whatthebleep.com.

Temple Grandin, 2012 Colorado State University, Fort Collins, Colorado, USA. http://www.colostate.edu/templegrandin, www.templegrandin.com.

Articles from CNN World, 2010 Cable News Network. Turner Broadcasting System, Inc. http://www.cnn.com/specials/2010/haiti.quake.

Articles from CNN Health, 2010 Cable News Network. Turner Broadcasting System, Inc. http://thechart.blogs.cnn.com/2010/10/27/cholera-cases-rising-around-the-world/.

Lacy, Marc. "Estimates of Quake Damage in Haiti Increase by Billions," February 16, 2010. Copyright 2010 The New York Times Company http://www.nytimes.com/2010/02/17/world/americas/17haiti.html?_r=0. Page no longer available except on archives.

"Who Needs Care?" The U.S. Department of Health and Human Services. http://longtermcare.gov/the-basics/who-needs-care/.

"Medicare," The U.S. Department of Health and Human Services. http://longtermcare.gov/medicare-medicaid-more/medicare/.

"Biggest cause of personal bankruptcy: Medical bills," June 25, 2013, *Today Money* published by Today.com, 2014 CNBC LLC. http://www.today.com/money/biggest-cause-personal-bankruptcy-medical-bills-6C10442408.

"The Field Trip Directory," © 2004-2012+ Family Publications, Ltd. http://www.classtrips.com/about-class-trips.

Jim Rohn Biography © 2014 Jim Rohn. http://www.jimrohn.com/jim-rohn-biography.

U.S. Bureau of Labor Statistics: http://www.usinflationcalculator.com/inflation/current-inflation-rates/.

Babauta, Leo. "Overwhelmed and Stressed? Do a Stress Assess," December 2014, Zen Habits published by Leo Babauta. Website: http://leobabauta.com/articles.

Newser Editors and Wire Services, "Exiled Dictator Returns to Haiti After 25 Years," January 6, 2011. © 2015 Newser, LLC. http://www.newser.com/story/109858/ exiled-dictator-returns-to-haiti-after-25-years.

Beaubuin, Jason. "Former Exile 'Baby Doc' Lands In Haiti Amid Praise," January 17, 2004. National Public Radio.org, 2014 NPR. http://www.npr.org/2011/01/17/133001394/former-exile-baby -doc-lands-in-haiti-amid-praise.

Brian Skoloff and Jane Wardell. "BP Oil Spill Cost Hits $40 Billion, Company Returns to Profit," November 2, 2010, Copyright ©2015 TheHuffingtonPost.com, Inc.: http://www.huffingtonpost .com/2010/11/02/bp-oil-spill-costs-hit-40_n_777521.html.

Haq, Husna. "BP oil spill 2010: How much will it cost?" May 3, 2010. The Christian Science Monitor © The Christian Science Monitor. http://www.csmonitor.com/Business/new-economy/2010/0503/ BP-oil-spill-2010-How-much-will-it-cost.

Bergin, Tom. "Special report: How BP's oil spill costs could double." December 1, 2010. Reuters U.S. Edition. © 2015 Thomson Reuters. http://www.reuters.com/article/2010/12/01/ us-special-report-how-bps-oil-spill-cost-idUSTRE6B02PA20101201.

REMEMBER TO DOWNLOAD YOUR BONUS ACTION GUIDE

Download your free copy of the Action Guide for *The RichLife: Ten Investments for True Wealth* at www.RichLifeActionGuide.com.